Research skills for students

Research methods **Brian Allison**
Planning a sample survey **Alun Owen**
Questionnaire design **Arthur Rothwell**
Research interviews **Tim O'Sullivan,
Carol Saunders, Jenny Rice**

**KOGAN
PAGE**

The Transferable and Learning Skills Series

Series editors:

Anne Hilton, Manager, Student Learning Development Centre, Library,
De Montfort University
Sue Robinson, Editor, Student Learning Development Centre, Library,
De Montfort University

Job hunting after university or college, Jan Perrett
Research skills, Brian Allison, Tim O'Sullivan, Alun Owen, Arthur Rothwell,
Jenny Rice, Carol Saunders
Successful group work, Simon Rogerson, Tim O'Sullivan, Jenny Rice,
Carol Saunders

First published in 1996

Reprinted in 1998, 2001   35 1443

Kogan Page Limited
120 Pentonville Road
London N1 9JN

British Library Cataloguing in Publication Data
A CIP record for this book is available from the British Library
ISBN 0 7494 1875 3

Design and typesetting by Paul Linnell, De Montfort University

Contents

Part C: Questionnaire design 69

Part D: Research interviews 100

Part A: Research methods

Aims

This part is designed for novices to research or for researchers with limited experience. Its aim is to provide you with an overview of the kinds of matters which can be examined through research and an introduction to the different kinds of research methods which are employed.

Objectives

By the time you get to the end of this part you should be able to answer the following questions.
- What is research?
- What constitutes a research question?
- What research methods and strategies are available?

Working through Part A

This part consists of two chapters:

1 Chapter 1 is designed to help you understand the *nature of research* and some of the issues which underpin the formulation of topics for research.

2 Chapter 2 is designed to inform you about the various *research methods* and strategies which are available. A review is included to enable you assess your familiarity with matters concerning research.

At the end of Chapter 2 (pages 24–26) you will find a *brief glossary of research terms*, which explains some of the specific research terminology you will encounter in the unit. You will find it helpful to work with a dictionary beside you so that you can define any words which are new to you.

Activities are included in this unit for you to carry out. These are designed to help you master the ideas which are being put forward and find information about research activities relevant to your interests. They will also help you to become informed about the range and nature of research which has been carried out in your college or university, particularly in your own subject field, as well as elsewhere. A number of these activities require you to use the library and other activities require you to talk to fellow students and university staff.

It is necessary for you to have access to a major academic library in order to work through this part. This is because one of the most important ways of learning about research is to read reports of research projects which have been completed and these are to be found mainly in libraries. A major reference source for summaries of research in all subjects held by most libraries is the ASLIB *Index to theses,* which is published annually and lists research projects completed for the award of research degrees (MPhil and PhD) in the United Kingdom.

It is assumed that you are skilled in using the library and fully conversant with the location of texts and journals relevant to your subject. If you have any difficulties in locating materials you should contact your local library.

Whenever possible, you should complete each activity before proceeding to the next section. However, it is appreciated that you may work on the unit elsewhere than in the library or even the university and, to help you make the most of the time when you are on university premises, some activities have been grouped so that they may be undertaken at the same time. This has been indicated on the activities. However, when activities have been grouped in this way, it is not advisable for you to proceed to a new section until all the activities in a group have been completed.

You should be.systematic in keeping a file of your responses to the activities as the discipline of maintaining full and adequate records is exemplary of research activity. You will also need your responses to some of the earlier activities in order to complete later activities.

1 The nature of research

Personal research

Research is a word which seems to be used more and more these days and, of course, it is used to mean many different kinds of things. Generally, it is used simply to mean 'finding out' something. Before buying, for example, a car, it would be sensible to find out which is the 'best buy' for the money that you can afford. This might entail reading the motoring journals or *Which* magazine, going round the car dealers looking at what is on offer and at what prices as well as checking out what kinds of bonuses or incentives the dealers have to offer, which might include the length of warranty offered and the kind of credit that is available. If you did such a survey thoroughly, you would have all the information it was possible to get in order to be in a position to decide what car to buy. However, the research you have carried out would never be able to tell you precisely which car to buy – all it can do is to put you in a position where you can make an informed judgement, which really means that you can decide by taking into account all the available evidence. Much of the daily decision making we do is based on this kind of 'finding out' research, whether it is about deciding what to cook as a meal when we have guests, what movie to see or which bank to put our money into. The research questions here are *What car to buy?*, *What food to cook?*, *What movie to see?* and *What bank to use?* In each case, we would have to decide what information is needed, how it can be collected, what factors are relevant and how the information can be used.

These examples all relate to *personal* research questions and, for the most part, it is unlikely that we would have to tell other people about them. Furthermore, because they are personal questions, it would not matter too much to other people if we make mistakes, collect inappropriate or unreliable information or if we make poor judgements on the basis of the evidence we have collected.

 Activity 1.1

> Identify three decisions you have made in the last two weeks which required getting some prior information. Write out the 'research questions' you asked yourself and then, in each case, list the factors you took into account, the information you thought was necessary, how you went about collecting it and how you weighed up the evidence in reaching the decision.

Professional research

Although research at a *personal* level is important to our everyday lives, this part is concerned with research at a *professional* level. Although professional research has much in common with the personal kind, it is carried out in a broader and more public context and so is expected to conform to standards which are understood and recognised by others in the professional field. In general, such research is characterised by being rigorous and systematic, is pursued through the use of appropriate research methods and invariably culminates in a report of some kind, which also needs to conform to accepted standards. These characteristics are embodied in the following definition:

> *Research is a systematic enquiry which is reported in a form which allows the research methods and the outcomes to be accessible to others.*

This definition contains elements which will be explained in this part.

Research questions

Research is a particular form of enquiry but, of course, any enquiry has to be an enquiry into something. It is not possible to do research without having a problem which needs to be solved or a question which needs to be answered.

> *Research is concerned with seeking solutions to problems or answers to questions.*

The problem or question constitutes the research topic. Identifying a topic which is worthy of enquiry and then formulating a meaningful research question or questions which can be answered are probably the most difficult parts of the research activity. It is worth spending a great deal of time formulating the research questions as it is a very real investment of time and effort. Being clear about what research questions are being asked is absolutely essential as, unless you are clear, a great deal of time and energy can be wasted collecting information which cannot be used. Carrying out the research is invariably a relatively straightforward matter once the question is clearly defined. It is axiomatic that 'an answer is only as good as the question', and a poorly constructed or vague question can only result in a poor or useless answer.

Questions usually begin with interrogatives such as 'What is…?', 'To what extent…?' or 'Does the…?' However, although questions may sound similar, they are often very different in the extent to which they can be answered. Some questions can be classed as *meaningful*, while others can be classed as *non-meaningful*. Questions are meaningful if they can be answered by enquiry and non-meaningful if they cannot be answered by enquiry.

A *meaningful* research question is one which is expressed in such a way that it indicates what it is that you will accept as an answer. At the simplest level, such a question might be:

> *'How high is the Eiffel Tower?'*

Height is a measurable variable and, therefore, the question implies that the answer would be a quantification or measure, which could be in feet or metres or, for that matter, in any unit of measurement provided it is specified, such as 'cricket bat lengths'. A more complex question might be:

To what extent is the frequency of library visits by third-year engineering degree students related to their performance in the final examinations?'

Clearly, a number of factors would need to be taken into account in a question like this but essentially the expected answer would be a statistical factor to support whether or not using the library could be considered to have any effect on examination performance.

The kinds of information to be expected in an answer to an historical research question such as:

'What social and economic factors led to the introduction of the 1870 Education Act?'

are implied by the question itself. For example, social factors such as population growth, the increase in industrialisation and urbanisation and the rise in social unrest would need to be taken into account, as would economic factors such as levels of taxation, increase in governmental responsibility for the costs of education and the increase in urban poverty.

 Activity 1.2

    a Write out three meaningful questions, one which involves a measure such as temperature, one which involves a relationship between two factors and one which involves possible causes of an event.

    b Ask two of your fellow students to read the questions and tell you what kinds of answers they would expect. Did what they say agree with what you intended?

Non-meaningful questions in research terms are those which are not answerable as a result of enquiry alone. These include metaphysical questions such as:

'Is there life after death?'

or judgemental questions such as:

'Was DNA a more important discovery than penicillin?'

5

Activity 1.3

    a Write out three non-meaningful questions relating to your own subject.

    b Ask two of your fellow students to read the questions and tell you what kinds of answers they would expect. Did what they say agree with what you intended?

Limitations of research

Research questions need to be meaningful but they also have to be feasible in terms of the time and resources available for the research as well as being within the abilities and experience of the researcher. A research project which can be carried out by a student during one semester is very different from that which can be carried out by a full-time professional researcher in a year or that carried out by a team of researchers in five years. *Feasibility* and *practicability* need to be taken into account when formulating research questions. A modest or even mundane research project which can be thoroughly carried out and reported is better than a large and complex one which, although it may seem a more exciting prospect, is difficult to carry out and is likely to end up with more questions than it started with. *Thoroughness of method* and *reliability of outcomes* are two of the most important characteristics of research and, indeed, if the world's knowledge can be compared to a wall, it has almost invariably been built with small but very soundly made and reliable bricks. Very few research projects result in earth-shattering outcomes such as the discovery of DNA.

Research is concerned with 'what is' and, sometimes, with 'what might be' – it cannot determine 'what ought to be'. 'What is' includes both description and explanation. Research is not concerned with the expression of your own beliefs, opinions and views, although, if you were carrying out a survey of some kind such as a study of students' attitudes to religion, it may be concerned with the opinions and views of others. It is, however, concerned with the collection and analysis of data which allows you to arrive at conclusions which are *valid* – that is, they are based on evidence which has been collected during the research. Of course, it is acceptable to put forward recommendations for future practice on the basis of the evidence presented and conclusions reached, but such recommendations or speculations are, in themselves, not part of the research.

2 The methods of research

Forms of research

There are different ways in which the world and human behaviour is viewed and understood. These differences are principally philosophical but they may also be religious and cultural. It follows that there are different forms of research which reflect the different standpoints. The forms of research described in this chapter can be placed under the general headings of positivism, which is principally based on positive facts and observable phenomena, and phenomenalism, which is principally concerned with the description and classification of phenomena. Although these forms appear to represent fundamentally different approaches, they are two aspects of the same endeavour and it must be emphasised that it is rare for any research project to rely exclusively on one form or the other.

Positivism

Research has its historical origins in science and most, but not all, research methodology in both the natural and social sciences subscribes to what has been termed the 'scientific method'. A primary goal of science and, therefore, research adopting the 'scientific method', is not only description but prediction and explanation. Initial investigations may lead to 'laws'. They depend upon the classification of similar substances and events and their observation. Consistencies or patterns in properties or behaviour are formed into descriptive laws which can then be used predictively. Laws, however, should always be regarded as tentative in so far as they may be changed or discarded as a result of subsequent investigation. At their highest level, the natural sciences seek explanations for these laws in terms of the underlying nature of reality. The level of explanation goes deeper as science develops. For example, the movement of the planets was first explained as being based upon a circle, then as epicycles on that circle, then as an ellipse around the sun. Newton explained this motion as resulting from gravity. Einstein explained gravity as a result of curved space-time. The natural sciences, which are concerned with the physical world, are based upon some fundamental characteristics of natural phenomena and these constitute basic assumptions about uniformity in nature which, consequently, underlie research.

The social sciences, which are concerned with human behaviour, may also depend on some degree of uniformity but, of course, not to the same level as that characterising natural phenomena. While the natural sciences, which can exert a high degree of control over the phenomena studied, can rely upon absolutes, research in the social sciences, which rest upon and recognise the variability of human behaviour, can only proceed on the basis of levels of probability. As a result, research in the social sciences which adopts the scientific method is based necessarily on certain assumptions or postulates about the uniformity of human behaviour. A postulate is something which is taken for granted. In general these are derived from the natural sciences and include the following:

a **The postulate of natural kinds**. This assumes that all instances in classes and categories of phenomena exhibit the same properties (eg all giraffes have long necks; all solid bodies are composed of atoms).

b **The postulate of constancy**. This assumes that phenomena remain the same or change very little or slowly over time (eg natural gas is a major source of energy supply in the United Kingdom; hedgehogs hibernate).

c **The postulate of determinism**. This assumes that there is an orderliness and regularity in nature and, therefore, there is a constancy in terms of cause and effect (eg rewards increase motivation; eggs break when you drop them). It is argued that if any phenomena falls outside the postulate of determinism then it is outside the realm of the scientific method.

Research in the sciences and research in the social sciences adopting the scientific method can generally be described as *positivistic* and is characterised by an absolute or varying level of generalisability. Because positivistic research frequently draws upon measurable evidence, it is sometimes referred to as *quantitative*.

Phenomenalism

In recent years some researchers, particularly those working in the social sciences, have taken the view that each and every phenomenon is unique and its uniqueness is its most important quality. In this view, every event is conditioned by variables such as time, location and culture, which are interactive, and, therefore, no two situations, by definition, can be identical and cannot be the basis for generalisation. To some degree, of course, this is a truism. The events which take place in a classroom on a particular occasion, for example, simply cannot be identical to those which take place in the same room on another occasion even though the same students and lecturer are present on both occasions. This research position does not rely on an acceptance of the three postulates described above and is generally referred to as phenomenological although sometimes the terms *naturalistic, qualitative* or *hermeneutics* are used.

Phenomenological research accepts that all situations are problematic to some degree and, therefore, the nature of the problems are revealed by examining the situation. Such research normally takes place in natural, 'everyday' settings and is not preceded by the formulation of research questions as in positivistic research, but anticipates that questions which are peculiar to the situation will arise during the period of the enquiry. Hermeneutics is a branch of phenomenological research directly addressed to the interpretive analysis of texts. The texts subjected to such interpretive analysis might be, for example, autobiographies, letters, versions of historical events or the plays of Shakespeare.

Phenomenological research is essentially inter-subjective on the part of the researcher and so both the content of the research and the means by which it is pursued are indicative of the researcher's intention. Furthermore, the researcher as observer is not only part of the phenomenon being studied but also exercises clear selection over what is observed. Such observation is essentially observer-oriented. The outcomes of observation in phenomenological research result in descriptions which are expressed as narrative and mainly in qualitative terms.

You will recognise, however, that these two research orientations are complementary rather than incompatible. Some kinds of information can only be expressed quantitatively (eg the actual number of students in a classroom) whereas there are aspects of any empirical enquiry which are necessarily and essentially qualitative (eg the learning ethos present in the classroom).

 Activity 2.1

Write down two main differences between positivistic and phenomenological research.

Research methodologies

The aim of this section is to give you a general overview of different research methodologies which can be adopted to address different kinds of research questions. By being familiar with all these different methodologies, an experienced researcher is able to identify the kinds of research questions which are implicit in a problem and will have the implications of the different methodologies in mind when formulating precise research questions. Of course, some researchers have a preference for one kind of research methodology over another and not only become expert in that method but tend only to address research problems which can be pursued by that method.

Each research method consists of a number of different stages, all of which are followed through systematically. The stages are listed sequentially for the sake of clarity although, in practice, it may be that they do not need to be followed consecutively. In all cases, it is assumed that the researcher will carry out a systematic review of all the relevant literature and that the outcomes of such a review will inform and underpin each stage in the research process.

As a general principle, planning how data will be used once it has been collected is an important part of any research design. Knowing how the data will be processed is essential to deciding not only what data to collect but also in what form it can be collected. There is little point in collecting a lot of data, no matter how interesting it is, and then having to ask what can be done with it! In positivistic or quantitative research it is assumed that quantifiable or numerical data will be submitted to statistical analysis. Instruction in statistics is not given here, but your library will have a selection of appropriate materials available.

When you come to the end of this section you should be able to identify the general characteristics of each of the different research methodologies and appreciate the significance and rationale of the individual stages in each. You should also be able to suggest which research methodologies would be appropriate in pursuing different research questions. It must be stressed, however, that these are only brief descriptions and for fuller explanations of the methods and the development and use of research instruments you will need to undertake further reading. Useful sources of information about research methodologies will be found in any academic library.

As with all academic disciplines, research has its own vocabulary and, although some of the words have general meanings, they have very specific meanings when used in a research context. The *Glossary* on pages 24–26 should be referred to in conjunction with the descriptions of the methodologies below.

The principal research methodologies to be described in this section fall under the following headings:

Research subscribing to the scientific method
Philosophical research
Historical research
Descriptive research
Experimental research
Phenomenological research
Practical research

It should be emphasised that while most research projects adopt one of these methodologies as a *main* form of enquiry, they invariably draw upon the other methodologies as essential parts of the enquiry. You should *not* assume, therefore, that any project must necessarily fit neatly into one of these types – research is demanding because it involves making decisions from among the available methodologies.

Research subscribing to the scientific method

The scientific method progresses from the initial identification of a problem through to a conclusion. Such progression is systematic, that is, a system is applied or imposed on the methodology in order to ensure an appropriate level of detachment on the part of the researcher and also that all relevant matters are considered and covered. The matter of detachment on the part of the researcher is important. In essence, a researcher is seeking the 'truth', however that may be defined, and is not setting out to prove his or her beliefs or opinions. The detached researcher arrives at conclusions on the basis of the evidence produced by the research and, therefore, accepts the outcomes of the enquiry, whatever they might be. This detachment is also evident in the way research is reported. A research report needs to be complete and accurate enough to enable other researchers to replicate the research, if they so wish, and arrive at similar conclusions.

The general stages in the 'scientific method' are:
a a 'felt difficulty' or the recognition of a problem;
b location and definition of the difficulty or problem;
c suggesting solutions to the problem. These normally take the form of hypotheses;
d deductive reasoning out of the consequences of suggested solutions or hypotheses;
e testing out the hypotheses by action.

These stages describe the general structure of the research process and are extended in practice depending on the nature of the research methodologies employed, which depend entirely on the nature of the questions being asked. You will recall that in Research questions on pages 4–5 emphasis was given to the importance of the question and the way it was expressed. A *meaningful* question was described as one which included a clear indication of the kind of answer which would be acceptable.

 Activity 2.2

Look back at the examples of Research questions which were given on pages 4–5. Sketch out the processes by which you might follow steps a–e above.

The way a question is framed dictates not only the kind of answer which would be acceptable but also the method of enquiry which is necessary to arrive at that answer. For example, questions of a philosophical nature require a philosophical research method, questions of an historical nature require an historical research method, and so on. In reality, most research projects ask more than one question and, similarly, most employ more than one research method. However, research projects are usually characterised by the principal research method used and it is accepted that other methods are employed as appropriate.

The four research methodologies described in this section are seen as subscribing to the scientific method. The stages in the scientific method, therefore, are the stages in each of the following research methodologies but these are expanded when this is necessary. Where appropriate, examples are given to illustrate elements in the methodologies.

Philosophical research

Research problems or questions are invariably expressed in language and all, to some extent, hinge on the meaning of terms or the way language is used. Being clear about 'what is' is fundamental to research and, when this is dependent upon an agreed understanding of how 'what is' is expressed, this often necessitates linguistic analysis and logic as described symbolically in language. Philosophical research, therefore, focuses on language, its interpretations, structure and meanings. Examples of language use, which has been the subject of philosophical enquiry, are the interpretations of the concept of 'freedom' and the layers of meaning attached to the word 'thermo-dynamic'. Some researchers and, indeed, some research questions, such as in aesthetics, are entirely concerned with the way language is used; however, for most purposes, the validity of philosophical research lies in its empirical application.

The stages in philosophical research are as follows:

a A 'felt difficulty'. An example of a problematic issue might be in the democratic ideal of providing increasing opportunities for the individual's 'free expression'. An important question, therefore, might be 'How free can expression be?'

b State hypothesis/es. A formulated hypothesis derived from this question might be 'The concept of freedom is not an absolute but requires identification of states of non-freedom or constraints on freedom.'

c Application of the concept in linguistic structures and an examination of its meanings. This involves a search for definitions and variety of applications in the literature, as well as a search for changes in meanings in relation to the contexts of its uses such as, in this example, legal, political and moral or religious contexts. To expand the example, does *freedom to* vote' really imply a *freedom from* specifiable restrictions, constraints or fears which inhibit voting'?

d Summation of meanings and applications to arrive at a *logical construct* in relation to the hypothesis. In the example, it might be deduced that the use of the concept 'freedom' must always be followed by an explicit statement of the constraints which need to be removed for freedom to be realised.

e Consideration of the implications and applications in practice. This may take the form of the 'if... then...' conclusion. The detachment and objectivity necessary to the research endeavour is demonstrated in philosophical research by the withholding of any value judgements. Following the example about the concept of freedom, a conclusion might be 'if freedom is to exist, then...', which would be a statement of the particular constraints otherwise inhibiting freedom in a particular situation or circumstance.

Activity 2.3

Write down a word or sentence relating to your own subject field which may be ambiguous or contentious and could form the basis of a philosophical question. List some of the implications of the problem, following stages **a–e** above.

Historical research

Historical enquiry begins when some event, development or experience of the past is questioned. You may recall that the third Research question posed, *'What social and economic factors led to the introduction of the 1870 Education Act?'* was an historical question.

An initial stage in historical research is to isolate the crucial points which give rise to the problem or uncertainty. This is followed by the formulation of a simple, clear and unambiguous description of the problem.

By definition, an historical problem cannot be pursued empirically; that is, you simply cannot go back in time and experience the events taking place. It is necessary, therefore, to rely on sources other than oneself. These are classed as primary or secondary sources although not all historical research might have access to both.

a **Primary sources** of information are those which are part of or directly related to the historical event. If the event being studied is within living memory, the primary sources might include, for example, the testimony of people able to be classed as reliable eye and ear witnesses. 'Oral history' is now becoming recognised as a particular kind of history, although much of this relies on people's memories of events, which might sometimes be suspect. Verbatim accounts of events recorded at the time (such as Hansard or court records) and original documents are also examples of primary sources, as are actual objects used in the past which can be examined first hand. Paintings, sculpture, architecture, furniture, tools, implements, clothing, pieces of equipment and so on fall into this category.

b **Secondary sources** of information are generally pieces of evidence at one or more stages away from the actual event. These include documents or records of some kind which give evidence of or about something which occurred, eg minutes of meetings, synopses of discussions, debates, newspaper reports, biographies and histories written by other historians.

While not wanting to confuse the issue, you can appreciate that what might be classed as a *primary source* for one kind of historical question might be classed as a *secondary source* for another kind of question. For example, Vasari's *Lives of the Great Painters*, published in 1568, would be a *primary* source if the question being pursued related to the ways art historians in different centuries were influenced by contemporary concepts of beauty, but it would be *secondary* source material if the question related to the working practices of a particular artist Vasari wrote about, such as Michelangelo.

 Activity 2.4

Reflect on the history of your own subject and write down some event or circumstance which you think could be illuminated by systematic enquiry.
- What sources of information would you need to use in order to pursue this enquiry?
- On which source would you rely the most?

Descriptive research

A large proportion of all research is descriptive research. This is because a clear statement of 'what is' is an essential prerequisite to understanding 'why it is so' and 'what it might be'. In a very real sense, description is fundamental to all research. Descriptive research sets out to seek accurate and adequate descriptions of activities, objects, processes and persons. Whenever possible and appropriate, such descriptions are rendered quantitatively as this enables statistical analysis to be made. It has been claimed that measurement is the cornerstone of research on the basis that anything that exists must exist in some quantity and, therefore, at least in theory, is able to be measured. In other words, the point is made that anything that is variable varies to some definable degree. This is obvious in variables such as height, weight, light, speed and colour, as they are able to be measured on standardised and commonly accepted scales. However, human attributes such as intelligence, happiness and personality characteristics as well as people's values and opinions, including such as those concerned with assessments of beauty and intensity of religiosity, are also variables and so, with more or less degrees of precision, are able to be measured quantitatively.

You will recall that, at the end of Chapter 1, it was stressed that research was not only concerned with description but also explanation. Descriptive research, therefore, is not only concerned with *fact* gathering but also with identifying and predicting relationships in and between variables.

The stages in descriptive research are as follows:
   a Examine the problematic situation.
   b Define the problem and state hypotheses.
   c List assumptions upon which the hypotheses and procedures are based.
   d Select appropriate subjects and source materials.

e Select or construct techniques for gathering data.
f Establish categories for classifying data – these need to be unambiguous, appropriate and capable of identifying similarities and differences.
g Validate data-gathering techniques.
h Make discriminating objective observations.
i Describe, analyse and interpret findings in clear and precise terms.

Descriptive research uses a variety of data-gathering techniques and instruments which range from the use of relatively simple tools such as stopwatches, weighing machines and rulers to very sophisticated devices such as chromotographic instrumentation and personality or attitudinal questionnaires and tests. Particular techniques and instruments can be used to overcome the human frailties of the researcher and so, for example, data collected from observations can be rendered more objective by the use of checklists or other devices, such as observation schedules. Any and all of the data-gathering techniques and instruments need to be characterised by the attributes of *validity* and *reliability*. *Validity* refers to authenticity and appropriateness of the content – for example, it is essential that an instrument actually measures what it sets out to measure. *Reliability* refers to the consistency of the technique or instrument – for example, it is essential that an instrument continually produces the same result when applied in identical situations on different occasions. A variable thermometer, for instance, would be of little use to anyone! There are many ways of testing the validity and reliability of instruments and techniques used in descriptive research.

There are many different forms of descriptive research and these fall into a number of main categories.

a **Surveys** are concerned with collecting data about the occurrence or incidence of events or instances in varying situations and circumstances. Surveys include enquiries into public views as expressed in opinions polls, product values as determined through market research, and school surveys (where studies might be made of settings, personnel and pupil behaviour, or attitudes), using survey tools such as observations schedules, questionnaires and interviews. Survey techniques are also employed in studies of the provision of human and material resources in, for example, libraries and laboratories, as well as in studies of specific behaviours, such as in job analysis and time-and-motion studies.

b **Case studies** are in-depth studies of particular events, circumstances or situations which offer the prospect of revealing understandings of a kind which might escape broader surveys. Case studies, particularly if chosen to represent instances which are different in degree although not in kind, tend to generate conclusions from the particular which may or may not be applicable to the general. Case studies can be made of any phenomenon ranging from individual people, groups and situations to material objects such as geological specimens and road traffic junctions.

15

c **Causal–comparative studies** typically set out to determine the relationships which exist between different factors, variables or dimensions in order to explain either their coincidence or their interdependence. A typical example of a causal–comparative study is the research into the incidence of levels of smoking and health failure. In this case the frequency and volume of two variables in a sample population are examined to determine their interrelationship or, in other words, by the comparison of two variables it is hoped to assess which of the two can be assessed as being the cause of the other.

d **Correlational studies**. Correlations are statistical relationships based on quantitative measures on two or more parameters. The parametric data used in correlational studies may be derived from the use of a variety of measuring techniques and instruments. Correlational studies are pursued on the same premise as causal–comparative studies but are dependent upon two or more variables being present as dimensions of the same phenomenon. In this case, measures on the two variables are correlated to assess the level of probability that they are interrelated. For example, from data acquired from a sample of smokers, it may be found that frequency of smoking correlated at a statistically significant level with personality factors as indicated by assessed levels of extroversion/introversion and neuroticism.

e **Developmental studies**. Development may be described as change which is assumed to occur over time as a consequence of factors such as growth, decay, maturation, education or experience. In developmental studies, comparisons are made between an initial state and one or more subsequent states in order to determine which factors could be deemed to be influential or responsible and to what degree. Typically, the two main kinds of developmental studies are *longitudinal* studies and *cross-sectional* studies.

Studies are *longitudinal* when the same subjects or phenomena are studied over a period of time. This would be the case, for example, in a study of changes in a building due to subsidence or weather over, say, a month or even years, during which measurements are systematically made at precise intervals of time. Another example would be the assessment of the educational achievement of a group of children as they grew older. Longitudinal studies invariably take a long time to carry out.

Cross-sectional studies are comparisons of subjects or phenomena at different stages in their development. In studies of this kind it is essential that the subjects or phenomena used to represent different stages of development are, to all intents and purposes, as identical as possible, in all respects except that of age. An example of this kind of study might be a study of a sample of a species of plant representing different stages in its growth. Another example might be a study of a sample of children of similar family background and educational opportunity at the ages of, say, ten, twelve and fourteen years of age.

f **Trend studies** are similar to developmental studies in that measurement or assessment of some state of affairs is recorded at varying intervals of time to determine the rate and direction of changes. An example of a trend study would be a comparison of the results of opinion polls made at different times in the run-up to an election. Another example would be the picture being built up of changes in the ozone layer in relation to the effects of CFC reduction.

 Activity 2.5

Identify three descriptive research projects in your subject field. In each case, write down the category of descriptive research and list the techniques and instruments which were employed. You may need to consult some research journals in your library to achieve this.

Experimental research

Whereas descriptive research seeks to answer the question *'What is?'*, experimental research seeks to answer the question *'What if?'* In essence, an experiment is when the researcher introduces some new element into a situation to observe the effects, if any, which that intervention produces. The purpose of experimental research is to identify causal connections. In an experiment, some of the relevant variables are controlled or held constant, whereas the other relevant variables are manipulated.

In the classic experimental research design, the subjects or phenomena being studied typically are divided into two matched groups, one of which is subjected to the experimental treatment and is defined as the *experimental group* and the other has no treatment and is defined as the *control group*. Prior to the experimental treatment being administered, both groups are tested on the relevant variables in what is termed the *pre-test*. At the conclusion of the treatment given to the *experimental group* both groups are tested again in what is termed the *post-test*. The results of both pre-tests and post-tests for both experimental and control groups are compared in order to assess the effects of the treatment on the experimental group.

By controlling some variables and manipulating others experimental research seeks to move into the area of prediction. One of its values is that it allows for controlled experimentation to assess possible effects before changes are made to a system and, of course, this would seem to be of most value when large systems, such as those in the health service or education, are involved.

The stages in experimental research are as follows:
   a Recognise the problem.
   b Identify and define the problem.

   c Formulate a problem hypothesis, deduce consequences and define basic
     terms and variables.
   d Select experimental variables.
   e Construct experimental plan:
     • identify all non-experimental variables and methods of control;
     • select subjects representing the population and assign to experimental
       and control groups;
     • select and validate instruments to measure performances;
     • outline procedures for data collection and analysis;
     • specify and validate nature of experimental treatment;
     • conduct pilot studies to refine procedures;
     • state statistical or null hypotheses.
   f Conduct experiment:
     • administer pre-test to experimental and control groups;
     • administer treatment to experimental group;
     • administer post-test to experimental and control groups.
   g Reduce raw data to allow examination of effect thought to exist.
   h Test for significance.

Experimental research characteristically is the deliberate manipulation of certain
factors under highly controlled conditions to ascertain how and why a particular
event or condition occurs. The degree and kind of control able to be exercised is of
critical importance and while, for instance, a high level of control in laboratory
conditions is able to be imposed in much science and technology research, it is much
more difficult to do this in social science research. Nevertheless, the quality of
experimental research is dependent upon the degree to which the variables are
controlled.

The key variables in experimental research are of two kinds – the *independent
variable* and the *dependent variable*. The dependent variable is the phenomenon
that appears, disappears or changes as the independent variable is applied. So, for
example, if it had been hypothesised that an individual's level of intelligence was
related to the intake of certain vitamins, the level of intelligence would be the
dependent variable and the intake of vitamins the independent variable. By controlling the intake of certain vitamins by an experimental group a comparison could then
be made with those of a matched control group to see if intelligence increased or not.
In order to be sure that it was the intake of certain vitamins (the independent
variable) that was making the difference to intelligence levels (the dependent
variable) and not some other cause, all other related variables, which might be
effective during the period of the experiment, such as other elements in the diet,
educational experiences or physical exercise, would need to be rigorously controlled,
that is, they would be the same for both the experimental and control groups.

Action research is a particular kind of intervention in a situation which has many of
the characteristics of the more usual experimental research described above. Action

research is typically a social science research methodology when the researcher, usually but not necessarily in collaboration with others, takes some specific action to improve practice, such as in a teaching situation. Because it is rooted in practice and sets out to address a specific problem in a specific situation, action research does not exercise control over the variables to the same level as would be the case with experimental research and neither is it likely to be able to arrive at generalisations which are applicable beyond the specific situation. However, because action research has a critical evaluative element and is most often undertaken in collaboration with others, it is able to feed back outcomes from the enquiry as it goes along and so is able to influence practices in a formative way.

In general terms, the stages in action research are the same as for experimental research, although they are not necessarily pursued sequentially. However, as action research is invariably a collaborative venture, critical issues relating to such matters as the formulation of hypotheses, identification of variables and the nature of the innovation or intervention are part of the ongoing discussion and negotiation with the other participants as the research progresses within the real life situation.

 ## Activity 2.6

Go through the research journals in your college/university library and identify *three* experimental research projects in your subject field. In each case, write down one of the hypotheses being tested and list the techniques and instruments which were employed.

Phenomenological research

Phenomenological research in general begins with the proposition that any situation, circumstance or event offers, in itself, a potential for illuminating enquiry. As phenomena lending themselves to such enquiry are invariably animate and time related, research adopting this method is predominantly in the social sciences. Despite the proposition that all phenomena have a potential for interesting enquiry, some are of more interest than others and, of course, individual researchers are more interested in some situations than others. The researcher adopting the phenomenological method, therefore, while not formulating precise questions prior to engagement in the research, as in that subscribing to the scientific method, nevertheless usually has a general feeling of the problematic nature of the situation to be studied.

Although phenomenological research does not have the same kind of discernible structure or method as that characterising research employing the scientific method, it still needs to be as rigorous and systematic in both implementation and reporting. Description is central to phenomenological research and, therefore, great emphasis

19

is given to the methods of recording events, circumstances and situations whether the phenomena being studied are real life situations or projections as in literature or film. The recording, in this sense, is essentially based in language and it follows that the resulting descriptions are, in fact, interpretations reflecting both the content of the event and the perceptual frame of the researcher/interpreter. Because phenomenological enquiry is based on the subjectivity of the researcher, two researchers may interpret the same event or phenomenon differently, both equally valid in this context.

In many circumstances, the presence of the researcher as observer affects the event being observed. This would certainly be the case if, for example, a researcher was observing a teacher working with a class of children in a school, where the very presence of the observer creates a different situation to that which would have been had the researcher not been there. In this case, the children's behaviour would certainly be affected by the researcher being in the room. To overcome some of the inherent problems in a situation like this some researchers take part in the event as a fully active participant, and so they themselves are part of the event being studied. This strategy is typically known as *participant observation* but, of course, when this strategy is being employed, ethical issues can be raised if the other participants are not aware of the study being carried out.

The outcomes of phenomenological research are invariably qualitative descriptions or interpretations, most usually in the form of narrative. Highly detailed descriptions are termed 'thick descriptions'.

 ## Activity 2.7

Go through the research journals in your college/university library and identify two phenomenological research projects in your own or another subject field. In each case, write down the topic of the research and the strategy adopted by the researcher.

Note: For the reasons given at the beginning of this section, it may not be possible to identify phenomenological research projects in some subject areas. If this is the case, you should make a note of this and move to the next section.

Practical research

While most research will continue to be in the familiar 'academic' modes, other ways of pursuing research are of growing importance. Practical research is not a research methodology in the sense of the ones described above. Rather, it describes an area of research resulting in a product or products, such as paintings, musical compositions, teaching packs or pieces of furniture, which constitute the main evidence of the research process.

Creative work in the arts and products resulting from such research may itself be seen as concrete evidence of systematic enquiry and result in contributions to knowledge, both in terms of product and process, which are accessible to others. It is principally the accessibility of the research process and the methodologies adopted which distinguishes practical research from simply the output of creative or practical people, such as artists, designers, engineers, composers or poets. In this, the definition of research given earlier: 'systematic enquiry which is reported in a form which allows the research methods and outcomes to be accessible to others' is critical in distinguishing what may be termed research from non-research.

Concomitant with other forms of research, practical research is directed towards the clarification or extension of understanding and knowledge. Both the process and the product are important in practical research. Clearly, the product is the principal outcome of practical research and this may take the form of, for example, an exhibition of paintings or sculpture, an industrial product or a musical composition. However, even if sometimes the product is highly original, innovative or creative, in the best sense of the word, it is rare that the work is sufficient in itself to communicate the nature of the research process or the methodology to others. An important element in practical research, therefore, is the form in which the relationship between the practical product and the research methodology is reported. Reports of practical research take a variety of forms other than that typified by the thesis or dissertation although a written research report may be part of the requirements for a research project submitted for an academic award.

Whatever the form in which it is reported and of which the product is part, a report of practical research sets out to convey clear expressions of:
- **the title**, which is a summary description of the topic pursued;
- **the purposes of the enquiry**, that is, the problematic issue which the research is directed to examine or resolve;
- **the methodology adopted**, which allows the stages in process to be distinguished in a systematic form in relation to the perceivable product;
- **the success and significance of the outcomes**, which may principally be the product, in relation to the initial purpose of the enquiry as well as to other existing or comparable forms.

It is important to note that, because of the individual nature of much of this kind of research, the possibilities of the research being able to be replicated and, therefore, verified, on the basis of the research report is not always appropriate or feasible in practical research. Nevertheless, practical research reports should be sufficient enough for some, if not all, of the research methodology to be replicated.

Activity 2.8

Identify two practical research projects in your own or another subject field. In each case, write down the topic of the research, the product or the principal outcomes of the research, and the strategy adopted by the researcher.

Note: For the reasons given at the beginning of this section, it may not be possible to identify practical research projects in some subject areas. If this is the case, you should make a note of this and move to the next section.

Overview of research methodologies

In most cases the title given to a project indicates, either explicitly or implicitly, the main research methodology adopted. Titles beginning with phrases such as *An experimental teaching strategy designed to...* or *A survey of...*, leave you in no doubt as to the main research methodology which underpinned the research. In contrast, it is not unusual to find titles such as *Property financing* or *Curriculum development*, which give no indication whatsoever about what was involved in the research. However, when researchers have taken great care in formulating a descriptive title, familiarity with the different research methodologies described in this chapter should enable you to deduce the kinds of question being asked from the titles given to a project.

For example, a research project with the title *The Resolution of Some Ambiguities in Scientific Concepts* is clearly an example of philosphical research, whereas *L. N. Cottingham, 1787–1847; His Place in the Gothic Revival* is an example of historical research. It can be inferred that *A Study of Senior Nurses – Demands and Conflicts* is descriptive research and a project titled *Improving the Knittability of Elastometric Yarn* is experimental research. Similarly, a project titled *An Investigation of the Therapeutic Relationship* would indicate phenomenological research and one with the title *Personalised Seating System for Disabled Adults* would suggest practical research.

From these examples you can see that it is possible in some cases to identify the main research methodology adopted in a project from the way the title is formulated *without you having any specialist knowledge about the actual subject matter of the project.*

◭ Activity 2.9

The titles given to 12 research projects drawn from a variety of subject fields are listed below. Using the appropriate code letter, write down the *main* research methodology which you think would characterise *each* project. *(Check your answers with the ones suggested on page 26).*

- Philosophical – P (there are two in this category)

- Historical – H (there are two in this category)

- Descriptive – D (there are three in this category);

- Experimental – E (there are two in this category)

- Phenomenological – PH (there is one in this category)

- Practical – PR (there are two in this category).

1 *The ethics of heterogeneity: modern Anglo-American feminism*
2 *Controversy in aesthetics: implications for teaching metacriticism in art education*
3 *The effects of pentamidine salts on phagocytic cell function*
4 *Current practice – garment designs*
5 *The development of reinforced flexible materials for use in medical situations*
6 *Women, class and representation in 19th century France*
7 *Critical study of* The Changeling
8 *A study of the long-term detention of those found unfit to plead and legally insane*
9 *The investigation and realisation of a fibre optic, high speed intra-car communication system*
10 *The impact of goat farming on hill vegetation in Scotland*
11 *The development of low environmental impact, high sucrose-yielding sugar beet by genetic engineering*
12 *Developments in the teaching of technology in pre-war Britain*

Review

Now that you have worked through the chapter, you should have a sound grasp of what is involved in research, be able to suggest what research can and cannot do, and be familiar with the terminology and the different methodologies which are available to the researcher.

There is no doubt that practice and experience in research is one of the most effective and efficient ways of learning about research in your field. However, until you develop appropriate skills and competencies in research, you should ensure that any research work you undertake is closely supervised by your tutor.

Brief glossary of research terms

In this chapter many research terms have been defined by the context in which they have been used. However, in addition to the research terms to which you have already been introduced, you may find the following terms useful when reading research literature at a general level. These are listed in groups to illustrate the relationships.

Subjects used in research

See also the definitions in Part B: Planning a sample survey.

- **Universe** – refers to all existing members of a stated class wherever they are, for example, all giraffes, all 16-year-old boys, all libraries, all turnips, in the world. .

- **Population** – a defined group within a stated class, such as all giraffes in British zoos, all 16-year-old boys in Birmingham, all libraries in universities in the UK, all turnips subjected to a particular fertiliser in Lincolnshire in 1992.

- **Sample** – a sub-group of a population selected according to particular criteria and taken to represent the whole group. The size of sample depends upon the size of the population and on ensuring that all the variables considered to be important are taken into account. A sample of giraffes, for example, would ensure a balance in relation to sex, age difference, length of time in captivity, variation in eating habits, and so on. A *random sample*, as the name implies, is a group chosen randomly from the population in such a way that each item has an equal or calculable chance of inclusion in the sample or, in other words, with no concern other than frequency, such as 'all boys selected on a random number basis from a list of surnames in alphabetic order of 16-year-old boys in Birmingham'. An *intact group* is a specific group usually chosen for convenience, for example 'all turnips taken from a specific field in Lincolnshire'.

- **Subject** – each instance in the given group which is being studied and on which data is being collected, for example each giraffe in the sample, each boy in the random sample and each turnip taken from the field.

Two key research concepts – 'variable' and 'hypothesis'

- **Variable** – characteristics of, or affecting, the phenomenon being studied which differ in measurable ways, such as frequency, time, age, temperature, strength of opinion, tension, and so each of these is called a variable. In experimental research, the independent variable is the experimental treatment (which might be, for example, the amount of fertiliser put on turnips) and the dependent variable is the characteristic which is affected (in the example this might be the weight of the turnip). The control of all other variables to ensure they are held constant (ie cannot affect the dependent variable) is essential in experimental research.

• **Hypothesis** – a proposition put forward as a basis for reasoning, described by some as 'a calculated hunch'. More technically, it is a deduction from the premises of a theory designed to be a test of that theory. Most frequently it is a statement that a relationship between variables exists, which is to be tested by enquiry. A null hypothesis is an inverted hypothesis and is expressed as a statement that the relationship does not exist. The rejection of the null hypothesis is a methodologically more acceptable way of showing that a relationship does exist and, therefore, accepting an hypothesis. In other words, 'innocent until proved guilty'.

Research techniques and instruments

a **Test** – an instrument designed to measure a variable. Tests take many forms depending on the variable being measured, for example red cell blood count or intelligence. A main goal of test construction is for the test to be *objective*, that is, independent of other factors, such as the possible effects of culture, language or home environment in the case of intelligence tests. *Standardised tests* are tests which have been subjected to widespread applications in varying situations to ensure stability and consistency. An extension of the standardisation of tests is the establishment of standards for certain conditions which are termed *norms*, against which individual performance can be compared. In the case of intelligence tests, norms have been established for widely different groups such as 12-year-old children, university students and airline pilots. The application of a test prior to an experiment is called a *pre-test*, and the application of the same test following the experimental treatment is called a *post-test*. The differences in scores on the pre-test and the post-test are used to determine the effects of the treatment.

b **Interview** – is a face-to face situation in which the researcher sets out to elicit information or opinion from a subject. Interviews can be structured, conducted according to a prearranged plan usually based on an interview schedule, or interviews can be unstructured, when the researcher can direct the questioning as the situation at the time might suggest is likely to be profitable. Questions may be open, being designed to encourage the subject to be expansive on a particular point, or closed, which only allow the subject to respond within a prespecified range of answers. Interviews enable the researcher to seek clarification on any points directly from the subject. See Part D: Research interviews.

c **Questionnaire** – has a similar purpose to the interview except that it is usually in printed form and may be completed without the presence of the researcher. All questionnaires are structured but the questions may be open, when the subject is required to write the answer in whatever form the subject wishes, or closed, for which the subject is required to select from a range of presented answers. Questionnaires are particularly useful when needing to procure responses from large samples as they can be sent out by post. Questionnaires do not allow for ambiguous answers to be clarified and, therefore, special care is taken to ensure the questions are expressed in such a way as to elicit answers which are meaningful. See Part C: Questionnaire design.

d **Observation** – is the observation and recording of events or circumstances in which the researcher is present. Observation usually focuses on specific aspects of the events or circumstances and schedules or checklists can be drawn up to aid both the observation and its recording. Observation usually aims to be detached and objective and so two observers of the same event, for example, could be expected to produce the same record. In contrast, participant observation is a form of observation in which the researcher intentionally becomes part of the situation being observed and, therefore, influential on the events being observed.

Activity 2.9 – solution

The titles suggest that the main research method characterising each project is as indicated below. Except in some obvious cases, of course, these may not be the methods underpinning the actual research projects.

1-P, 2-P, 3-D, 4-PR, 5-E, 6-H, 7-PH, 8-D, 9-PR, 10-D, 11-E, 12-H.

Part B: Planning a sample survey

Introduction

This part is aimed at anyone considering undertaking a sample survey who has little previous experience of doing so. It aims to improve your awareness of the things you can do, as well as highlighting some of the potential pitfalls and ways to avoid them, after which you should be able to plan and undertake a more effective sample survey.

Most of the key ingredients for performing a successful survey are covered, but with the emphasis on the basics. It should therefore provide enough detail for most undergraduate research. The use of statistical theory is deliberately avoided to keep the focus sharply on survey methodology, although part of the role that statistics plays in sample surveys is outlined for you to follow up where appropriate.

Objectives.

After working through the exercises in this part, you should be able to:
- explain the meaning of some of the basic jargon used in sample surveys;
- distinguish between and describe some of the alternative approaches for conducting a sample survey;
- select an appropriate approach for conducting your survey;
- describe the benefits of and undertake a pilot survey;
- give examples of some of the common problems encountered with sample surveys, and tips to avoid them;
- plan and undertake a more effective sample survey.

How to proceed

It is assumed that you are hoping to undertake a sample survey. Some of the activities, therefore, relate to your own sample survey: if you do not have a survey in mind, then you can ignore these particular activities. Each chapter builds on the work of previous ones, and it would be best to study the part in this order, but at your own pace.

 Preliminary activity

In Chapter 11, the Bibliography, are two additional sections:
- a pro forma of a *survey plan*, which is to be used as a working document and completed as you work through the activities. (You may wish to copy it out for rough work initially.)
- a number of *survey examples,* some of which are based on real surveys that have been conducted. These will be used in many of the activities as a basis for discussion.

---

3   Where should you start?

A typical approach

Below is a flow chart which shows a poor but all too common approach to undertaking a sample survey.

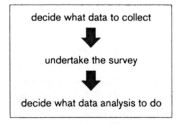

```
decide what data to collect
          ⬇
   undertake the survey
          ⬇
decide what data analysis to do
```

Problems with this typical approach
No initial thought is given to the aims of the survey. As a result, the information/data may not be appropriate (eg wrong data collected, or data collected on wrong subjects, or not enough data collected). Consequently, you may not be able to do the data analysis you would like.

 The library loan survey (survey example 1, page 65)
Suppose we simply went ahead and only recorded the number of times each book in the sample was borrowed during the year. After conducting the survey we might wonder whether or not there are any differences in the loan rates between various degree courses. If we had not thought about recording the courses that the students borrowing the books were on (assuming of course this is available), we could not do this analysis.

A better approach

The flow chart below shows how it perhaps should be done.

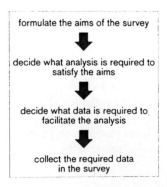

```
formulate the aims of the survey
              ⬇
decide what analysis is required to
        satisfy the aims
              ⬇
decide what data is required to
       facilitate the analysis
              ⬇
   collect the required data
       in the survey
```

The key point is the order in which things should come. You should formulate the aims of your survey and decide what data analysis is needed right at the beginning.

 With the library loan survey, having formulated the aims of the survey, we would have realised that we wished to compare courses. Therefore, for each book, we know we would need to record not only the number of borrowers, but also the course each of those borrowers was on.

 Activity 3.1

You will see that each of the survey examples has an aim(s). Jot down the aim(s) of your survey, and perhaps make a note of the title and the location(s) of your survey.

If you haven't already thought of how you are going to analyse your data, you should do one of the following:

- Give the data analysis some thought and come back to this part later.
- Leave the decision over which data to collect until you have worked through this part, but still give it the thought it requires before you conduct the survey.

4 Sample survey jargon

Before we move on to look at methods of conducting your survey, we need to explain some basic jargon. This will allow us to talk more easily about sample surveys and allow you to thumb through some of the references given in Chapter 11, the Bibliography.

Some basic jargon

Subject (or element)
Either of these words is used to refer to whatever it is you are hoping to obtain information about or from.

 Since a lot of sample surveys are conducted on human populations, the subject is often individual people. This is the case in the pre-election poll (survey examples B and C on pages 65–6). For the library loan survey, the subject is a book.

Sample
This is the group of subjects from whom you actually intend to collect information, by interviewing, observing or measuring, etc.

Population
The population is the larger collection of all the subjects, from which your sample was drawn, that you wish to apply (statisticians use the word infer) your conclusions to.

 Activity 4.1

For each of the survey examples, have a go at jotting down what you think the subject is. The first two have been done for you. See Appendix 1, page 55, for the solution.

Survey example	Subject
A	*Book*
B	*Person*

 Activity 4.2

On your survey plan, state what the subject is for your own sample survey. Leave the population for now, as shortly we will see that this requires further thought.

Target population and study population

There are really two populations that exist within your survey, and understanding how they relate to each other is the key to obtaining a sample which is representative of the population.

- The *target* population is the population from which you would like to obtain a sample and to which you would like to apply your conclusions.

- The *study* population simply consists of subjects whose characteristics are similar to those of the subjects in the sample. In other words, the sample is always representative of the study population.

A pictorial view of how the sample relates to the target and study populations.

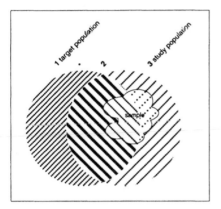

Notice how the sample is inside the study population, ie the sample is a small part of the study population. The sample is not necessarily inside the target population, ie there may be subjects in the sample who are not in the target population. You need to make sure as far as possible that the subjects in your sample are part of your target population.

Make sure your sample consists of subjects whose characteristics are likely to reflect those present in the target population. Sometimes a difference between the target and study populations exists, because gaining access to certain subjects in the target population might not be easy or even possible.

Consider the library survey. Suppose we decide to take a sample of books from one part of the library only. (Note that the short-loan books are in another part, and these might be borrowed more frequently than other books.) We still hope to infer from this sample what the average number of loans per year is for the library as a whole. The target population consists of all the books in the library including short-loan books. However, the study population excludes short-loan books since none will be included in the sample. Since the short-loan books are probably borrowed more often than

31

most books in our sample, the results of our survey would give a mean borrowing rate that is too low. Our sample is not representative of the target population.

 Consider the customer profile survey (survey example E, on page 66). Assume that those customers who have not purchased anything have declined to take part in the survey. The survey was intended to provide the views of both purchasing and non-purchasing customers. The target population was to be all customers, but the study population would be only those customers who made a purchase. Since there may be reasons why a purchase was not made, these non-purchasing customers could well have different views to those who did purchase. So the answer is probably no. Again, the sample is not representative of the target population.

In both of these examples, the target population is who/what you had intended to conduct your survey on, and perhaps write a report about. However, it is important that you remember that you can apply your results only to the study population.

 Activity 4.3

Have a look at surveys C and K (on pages 65 and 68) in the survey examples. The target population was described in each case. Have a go at briefly describing the study population and indicate how this differs from the target population. See Appendix 1 on page 55 for the solution.

 Activity 4.4

Now think about and try to describe the potential target population for your own sample survey. If you find this too difficult, leave it for later on.

Ask yourself whether or not there is likely to be any part(s) of this target population that you may not realistically be able to get access to. Also, think about whether you will be including any subjects who are not really part of the population you wish to survey. Jot down any thoughts you have and, in light of these, modify your *target population* (if required) and enter the details for the target population in the survey plan.

Sampling frame and sampling unit

Sampling frame
This is a list of all the subjects or sampling units making up the population.

- A list of people's names that make up the population from which you wish to obtain a sample, eg a local electoral register, employment records.

- A list of addresses for the area from which you wish to obtain information. The post office can provide a database of post-coded addresses (at a cost) for any area. A–to–Z guides give such a list for small areas and town plans may also prove useful.

- The telephone directory is a well-used sampling frame for conducting surveys by telephone.

- A map could be your sampling frame, if you are selecting a sample of areas or streets to survey.

- In the case of the library loan survey the sampling frame is a list of books in the library.

However, the sampling frame is needed so that your sample can be selected at random from the list. Therefore, in practice, a sampling frame is only required when you need a random sample.

 Activity 4.5

From the survey examples, only D (page 65), G and H (page 67) used a sampling frame. Have a go at jotting down what you think these sampling frames were. You don't need to be specific, for example simply state a list of books in the library. See Appendix 1 on page 56 for the solution.

Sampling unit
The subjects are sometimes grouped together into what are referred to as sampling units. The reason for using this term is that we often have a list of sampling units but not a list of the individual subjects. Therefore, it is usually more sensible or convenient to choose your sample by selecting from the list of sampling units.

In the pre-election poll, the sample is constructed by deciding which households to visit and not which people to interview. The sampling unit in this case is a household, while the subject is the person in the household who is to be interviewed.

The sampling unit and the subject are often the same thing. This is the case with the library loan survey, where the subject and the sampling unit would both be individual library books.

Summary

We have met the following words, which you should be able to explain in the context of sample surveys and also relate to your own sample survey:
- subject
- sample
- target population
- study population
- sampling frame
- sampling unit.

Alternative explanations can be found in Part A: Research methods.

5 Sample designs

About this chapter

Now that you are familiar with the jargon, the next thing we need to do is decide which subjects from our population should be in the sample. There are a number of methods, referred to as sample designs, that you can use to do this. Some of these can be complicated to describe, so we will look at the following relatively straightforward but still popular designs:

- simple random sampling
- systematic sampling
- stratified sampling
- quota sampling
- cluster sampling
- judgemental sampling
- convenience sampling.

Having done this, in Chapter 6 we will look at choosing a design appropriate for your survey. However, if you feel that you have an idea as to which of the sample designs might be appropriate, then by all means go straight to that one and study it.

Simple random sampling

The basic idea

We obtain a sampling frame, number each subject in the frame 1, 2, 3, and so on, choose some numbers at random (in our range) and include in the sample those subjects whose numbers match these random numbers. This allows every subject an equal chance of being included in the sample, which means there is usually a good chance of getting a representative sample.

 Using simple random sampling for the library loan survey, we would do the following to select randomly the books to be included in our sample:

    a Obtain a definitive list of all the books we wished to sample from (ie the sampling frame). This could be an inventory of the books kept by the library.

    b Give each book a unique reference number. Assuming there are 1,000 short-loan books and 8,000 normal-loan books, we could number the short-loan books from 1 to 1,000, and the normal-loan books from 1,001 to 9,000. Alternatively, we could use an existing numbering system if there is an appropriate one in use.

    c Generate a sequence of numbers at random in the range 1 to 9,000. These numbers are referred to as random numbers (more on this in a moment).

d Use the random numbers we have generated as the reference numbers of the books we choose for our sample.

Random numbers

Random numbers can be found in tables of random digits from booklets of statistical tables, such as those in Neave (1978), or at the back of most introductory textbooks in statistics. There is a table of random digits in Appendix 2 on page 58, which simply consists of row after row of single digits between 0 and 9, grouped into sets of four for ease of reading.

The process of generating random numbers, and even of selecting subjects using these numbers, can be done by computer. In fact, the table of random digits in Appendix 2 was generated using the following commands from the statistical analysis package called MINITAB:

MTB> Random 40 c1-c5;
SUBC> Integer 0 9.

Continuing with our example of the library loan survey, we need to generate random numbers that are all between 1 and 9,000. Suppose we choose a random starting position in the table in Appendix 2, say third column (a column being a block of four digits), eleventh row (we could have started anywhere). Our first set of four digits is therefore 6063. We now read along left to right (you could go up or down or right to left!), splitting the digits into sets of four-digit random numbers.

We therefore obtain the following random numbers:

6063 9092 7714 3666 3508 5780 1895 0790 7323 4423 3081 5453 4170 2129 0968
0241 5352 4232 2771 8996 6001 3626 1482 5950 9171 4925 6965 7104 7053 4002
9964 4851 3318 5345 2202 8242 0447 8455 3094 5250 3482 0392 7741 0316 8547
9874 3798 5086 2347 9983 1426 3153 2471 9029 0101 9602 0868 3173, etc.

Q Why do you think we used four-digit random numbers?

A So that we can get numbers in the range 1 to 9,000.

We ignore any random numbers that are greater than 9,000, because we do not have books with a number above this. For example, the second number, 9092, is ignored because no book with such a number exists. If we wanted only a very small sample of ten books in our sample then we would generate ten of these random numbers. Therefore the first ten relevant random numbers from the tables would be:

6063 7714 3666 3508 5780 1895 0790 7323 4423 3081

You may need initially to generate more random numbers than you require, to account for the fact that some of them may need to be ignored.

 Activity 5.1

Repeat the example of selecting ten books for the library loan survey, but this time beginning on column 2, row 5 of the random number table. See Appendix 1 on page 56 for the solution.

A common mistake is to think that simple random sampling can be achieved by choosing subjects from the sampling frame themselves, using judgement to make the selection random. This is not the case! Most people using this technique will not select two subjects that are side by side or follow each other on the list, so that each subject does not in fact have an equal chance of being included.

Summary

You have seen that to obtain a simple random sample you need to:
- obtain a sampling frame;
- number each sampling unit;
- generate a sequence of random numbers;
- use these random numbers to select the sampling units.

Systematic sampling

The basic idea

Systematic sampling has similarities with simple random sampling, except that the only random selection involved relates to which subject we select as our first one from the sampling frame. We then select further subjects for our sample by including say every tenth subject, or every twentieth or using whatever gap is required to meet the required sample size and cover the whole sampling frame.

 Using systematic sampling to select the books in our sample for the library loan survey, we would do the following:
  a Generate a list of books as we did with simple random sampling (ie a sampling frame).
  b Randomly select the first book in our sample from the first part (more on this in a moment) of the sampling frame.
  c Choose further books to make up our sample, by selecting books at equal intervals down the list.

Since we cannot include in our sample any books that occur before the first selected book, we don't want it to be too far down our list. If we wanted 100 books in our sample from the 9,000, we should choose books at intervals of 90. This is calculated as follows:

$$\frac{\text{No. of sampling units}}{\text{Sample size}} = \frac{9000}{100} = 90$$

Therefore, we need to make sure our first book is randomly selected from the first 90 books (ie from those numbered 1 to 90). We do this by randomly selecting a two-digit random number. If the number is above 90 we ignore it and select another until we obtain one that is in the range 1 to 90. Suppose we generated 60 as our random number, our first book is then book number 60 on our list.

We would then have the following books in our sample:

```
  60  150  240  330  420  510  600  690  780  870
 960 1050 1140 1230 1320 1410 1500 1590 1680 1770
1860 1950 2040 2130 2220 2310 2400 2590 2680 2770 etc.
```

Activity 5.2

Refer to the customer profile survey (survey example E). If there are 99 customers that day, and we wish to interview 10 of them, which of the first 99 customers do you think should be interviewed? Use the random number starting on row 20, column 10. See Appendix 1 on page 56 for the solution.

The big problem with systematic sampling is when the subjects are listed in the sampling frame in some sort of periodic order. For example, suppose for simplicity the books occur in the sampling frame grouped into topic areas (I avoid the word subject for obvious reasons). Suppose there are ten books per topic and within each topic area the books are listed oldest to newest. If we then select books 1, 11, 21, etc we would have the oldest books possible in our sample, which is not likely to be representative.

There are, however, certain ways in which the subjects can be grouped in the sampling frame, which suggest systematic sampling is preferable to simple random sampling. Raj (1972) gives some further examples on this.

Summary

You have seen that to generate a systematic sample you need to:
- perhaps obtain a sampling frame (note we didn't need one in Activity 5.2);
- determine the interval between sampling units using the following formula:

$$\frac{\text{number of sampling units}}{\text{sample size}}$$

- select the first sampling unit at random from the first group of sampling units in the sampling frame. The number of sampling units in this group is the same as the interval size calculated above;
- select further sampling units at each interval down the list.

Stratified sampling

The basic idea

Stratified sampling is used when the population is thought to consist of a number of smaller sub-groups, or sub-populations, such as male/female, different age/ethnic/ interest groups, which are thought to have an effect on the data to be collected. These sub-groups are called *strata* (strata being plural for *stratum*). The idea is that the sampling units in any particular stratum are as alike as possible.

Once the strata have been identified, a simple random sample is taken from each stratum separately. The resulting *stratified sample* is then more likely to reproduce the characteristics of the population.

Eg For the foot measurement survey (survey example 2 on page 61), age and sex are known to affect foot dimensions. Therefore, stratified sampling could be used. On the following page is the sort of information you could perhaps obtain on the age/sex distribution of a country. There are 14 age groups in each of the two sex groups, giving a total of 28 strata.

> **Q** Once you know how big the overall sample is to be, how do you decide how to allocate this between the strata (we refer to this as allocating the sample)?

> **A** There are a number of methods of allocating the sample, of which two are reasonably straightforward:

Equal allocation simply means making the sample size in each stratum the same. For example, if we required an overall sample size of 10,000 in the foot measurement survey, we would require 10,000/28 = 357 (or more likely 350) in each stratum.

Proportional allocation provides sample sizes such that the proportion of the overall sample size in each stratum reflects the proportions in the population.

Population of Taiwan by sex and age in 1989 (000s)

Age	Total	Male	Female
0–4	1,602	830	772
5–9	1,950	1,005	945
10–14	1,975	1,016	958
15–19	1,814	929	885
20–24	1,916	982	934
25–29	1,972	1,011	961
30–34	1,843	941	902
35–39	1,604	818	785
40–44	1,020	521	499
45–49	913	464	449
50–54	825	415	410
55–59	769	416	353
60–64	708	415	293
64+	1,197	636	562
Totals	**20,107**	**10,399**	**9,709**

Source: Office of Statistics, Taiwan.

Note: due to rounding, values may not add up exactly.

Eg As an example of proportional allocation, suppose for a foot measurement survey of Taiwan we wanted to have a total sample size of 5,000 people. How many males aged 0–4 years should we include?

There are 830,000 males aged 0–4 years out of a population of 20,107,000. This is 4.128 per cent, so we would want 4.128 per cent of the 5,000 subjects in the sample in that particular stratum, ie we would want 206 males aged 0–4 years in our sample.

In actual fact, to use stratified sampling, we would need to select the males aged 0–4 years at random from a list of the population! This is never going to be possible or practical. Therefore, we would probably measure those males aged 0–4 years who are accessible to us – we are then not using stratified sampling but something called quota sampling, which we will be looking at very shortly.

Neyman allocation

This is another very popular method for allocating the sample and Anderson et al. (1993) and Raj (1972) give good accounts. Sheaffer et al. (1990) also gives an extension to the Neyman allocation, which considers the relative costs of obtaining data from each stratum.

 Activity 5.3

Using the information on the population distribution of Taiwan, and using proportional allocation, calculate how many subjects should be in some of the other 27 strata (recall the total sample size is to be 5,000). There is no need to do this for all the strata, just enough to get the hang of the calculations. Check your answers (with Appendix 1 on page 57) one by one as you go along until you are happy.

Summary

You have seen that to obtain a stratified sample, you need to:
- obtain a sampling frame;
- identify the strata;
- allocate the sample size to the various strata (this may require information relating to population breakdown by the strata);
- generate a simple random sample for each strata.

Quota sampling

The basic idea

Quota sampling is very similar to stratified sampling, the only difference is that with quota sampling we do not choose a simple random sample from each strata. Instead, we accept whatever subjects are accessible to us, as long as they come from the sub-groups we have identified.

Normally we would not use the term strata in the context of quota sampling, so we revert to the term sub-group.

Quota sampling is so called because the number of subjects required in each sub-group of the sample is referred to as the *quota* to be obtained. The proportion of the sample in each sub-group is usually constructed to reflect those in the population.

 In the foot measurement survey example, the sample size in each sub-group would be calculated the same way as before for stratified sampling. However, instead of selecting the subjects to be included in the sample at random from a sampling frame, they are chosen by visiting people at work, at school, or at home and so on, until the quota in each sub-group has been filled. It is usually the more accessible subjects that are used to make up the quotas.

A tally sheet is a popular way of monitoring the progress towards reaching the desired quotas. (See Appendix 3 on page 59 for an example that could be used for the foot measurement survey.)

Summary

You have seen that to obtain a quota sample you need to:
- identify the sub-groups;
- allocate the sample size to the various sub-groups (this may require information relating to population breakdown by the sub-group);
- obtain the sample by using the most accessible subjects from various sub-groups until quotas are complete.

Cluster sampling

The basic idea

Cluster sampling involves splitting the population into sub-groups called clusters. However, unlike stratified sampling and quota sampling, in which the subjects in a particular stratum or sub-group are meant to be as alike as possible, the idea is to have the various characteristics that the population might contain represented in each cluster.

Cluster sampling is commonly used when the population covers an area that can be divided by regions, eg dividing an area to be studied into a number of streets, or dividing the city into postal districts. A small number of these clusters are selected at random (using simple random sampling). Every subject in the chosen clusters is then included in the sample.

 A cluster sample could be obtained for the library loan survey, by considering the shelves in the library as clusters. A simple random sample of shelves is then selected, and all books that are kept on those particular shelves are included in the sample.

In this case, cluster sampling would probably not give a representative sample, since we cannot be sure that each shelf contains similar profiles of book borrowing.

One key problem with cluster sampling is choosing appropriate clusters. For example, how big should the clusters be? Scheaffer *et al.* (1990) give a good discussion on this issue.

Judgemental sampling and convenience sampling

Judgemental sampling

Subjects are included in the survey in such a way that they are thought to be representative of the population. This has similarities with quota sampling, except that no sub-groups are identified, and no particular quotas are required.

 We could take a judgemental sample for the library loan survey, by looking at the number of date stamps on the inside cover of some of the books, selecting some that appear to be borrowed quite often, some that appear to be borrowed less often etc.

Convenience sampling

A convenience sample simply includes those subjects that are immediately to hand.

 With the library loan survey we could take one row of books from the first shelf we come to. As another example, a survey of students could be done using just the students in one class.

Summary

 Activity 5.4

Make a list of the sampling methods covered in this chapter and, for each of the survey examples, see if you can decide which sample design was used. The solution is provided on page 57.

6   Selecting a sample design

Measuring the accuracy of your survey results (margins of error)

Before looking at how you should proceed with choosing an appropriate sample design, we need to consider the issue of accuracy.

Usually, one of the aims of a survey is to estimate what are referred to as population parameters, such as the mean average value for a particular variable. In other words, you may want to use the mean from the sample as an estimate of the mean for the population. For example, in the library survey, you may wish to measure the mean number of loans per book per year from the sample and use this as an estimate for the whole library.

But how can we say how accurate the results are? (That is, how close is the sample mean to the mean of the population?)

We can never say exactly, because we will never know the *true* mean value for the population. However, if we use one of the sample designs (from Chapter 5) that involves random selection then we can use statistical theory to calculate various statistical measures such as standard errors and confidence intervals. These give a kind of estimate of the *margin of error* in the results. Anderson *et al.* (1993) give a good basic guide to this in the chapter on sample surveys.

If you do not require the calculation of these margins of error, then any of the sample designs can be used.

Choosing a sample design for your survey

The decision as to which design to use can be made in two stages. In Stage 1 you consider what is *required* in order to use a particular design (and whether you can meet those requirements), as well as what each design can *provide* you with (and whether this provides you with what you want).

The main requirements of some designs are:
- sampling frame;
- access to subjects selected at random from the sampling frame;
- information on the population to divide it up into strata, sub-groups or clusters.

You may need the design to provide:
- a representative sample;
- calculation of margins of error (see Measuring the accuracy of your survey results, above);

• ability to report results for particular sub-groups in the population.

 Activity 6.1

Before we look at stage two of this decision-making process, have a think about which design(s) may be appropriate for your survey. Remember to consider whether you have available what the design requires and whether the design provides you with what you need. Jot down any thoughts you may have.

Having decided which design(s) seems suitable, in Stage 2 you consider the practicalities involved in using the design(s).

You need to consider issues such as:

a **Cost: time and money**
Some designs take more time than others to plan and undertake. Stratified sampling and simple random sampling can be time consuming because of the need to generate the sample randomly. Quota sampling is usually a less time consuming and cheaper alternative to stratified sampling, because you do not need to select the subjects randomly. Systematic sampling is quicker to use than simple random sampling. Cluster sampling is a useful way of saving time if your subjects are spread over a large area.

The list below indicates some of the costs you need to bear in mind:
• planning the survey;
• developing the data collection form;
• printing and copying the data collection form;
• undertaking a pilot survey (see Chapter 8);
• making modifications to the survey plan if required;
• first attempt at data collection;
• subsequent attempts at data collection;
• data entry;
• data checking;
• data analysis;
• preparation of report.

To cost your survey as a whole, try to cost each task individually in terms of time and money and total them up. The pilot survey is a good tool for estimating some of the costs in the collection of the data, as well as perhaps data entry.

If you are collecting data by calling on people in their homes you will need to make time allowances because of subjects declining to participate, and for

45

making further calls if no one is at home. Typically, expect no more than 50 per cent of the subjects to be at home during your first attempt. You will probably get about half of the remaining 50 per cent at the next call, and perhaps about half of the now remaining 25 per cent at the third call.

b Physical practicalities
Designs that involve random selection provide the best sort of sample, but they might not be practical if the subjects you select are not easily accessible. For example, if having planned your survey using stratified sampling (so that you can obtain information on sub-groups and calculate margins of error) you cannot get to the subjects selected using a reasonable amount of effort and money, then perhaps you should consider quota sampling.

c Having the expertise/confidence to use a particular design
If having worked through this part, and perhaps doing further reading, you still haven't got to grips with, for example, stratified sampling, then use a design you are confident with, or seek assistance.

Combining several designs

This is what you may well need to do in practice. For example, the anthropometric (foot measurement survey) combined the use of cluster sampling and quota sampling. The country was divided up using areas as clusters; some of these clusters were selected at random and a quota sample then obtained from each of the chosen clusters.

 Activity 6.2

Take some time now to reconsider your thoughts in Activity 6.1 on which sample design(s) to use. You may wish to look back at some of the earlier comments on the practicalities of using a particular design.

The survey plan on pages 63–64 has a space for details relating to your sample design. Write down any thoughts/ideas you may have for completing that section. (See Appendix 4 on page 59 for examples of completed survey plans that may help give you an idea of what to write.) However, there is no need to enter this information in your survey plan just yet.

7 Data collection methods

Some commonly used methods

Have you thought yet about how you are going to collect your information? The following gives a flavour of some of the possibilities.

a By post

If you are thinking about using this method, it is important that questionnaires are clear and unambiguous.

Advantages
- Can help to reduce costs.
- Useful if the sample is spread over a large geographic area.
- Can be used to ask questions that may not be appropriate asked face-to-face, or questions that require a considered answer.

Disadvantages
- Response rate is likely to be poor (ie high non-response, more on this in a moment).

Further information
- See Part C: Questionnaire design.

b By telephone

Advantages
- Telephone directory is a readily available sampling frame.

Disadvantages
- Need to be careful about the exclusion of subjects not listed in directory. Random digit dialling is a common way of including ex-directory subjects, although non-telephone owners are still excluded.
- Can be time consuming.

Further information
- Frey (1989) is an excellent source of information on telephone surveys.

c One-to-one interviews (at home, in the high street, etc)

Questions need to be written down and asked in a consistent manner, with elaboration given only if really pushed. This is to keep it consistent from subject to subject. If calling at households, it is best to interview only one person per household, since there seems to be evidence that attitudes would be similar (positive correlation between attitudes and household).

Advantages
- Usually provides a higher response rate, although you need to count subjects who decline to take part as 'non-responders'.
- Ambiguities in the questions asked can be clarified.

Disadvantages
- Can be time consuming.
- Need to be sure that if there are several interviewers they are consistent in their questioning.

Further information
- Part D: Research interviews gives some useful advice on conducting one-to-one interviews.

d Mall interviews

These involve setting up a table/focus point possibly with a display. Subjects come to you to see what it is about and hopefully agree to participate.

Advantages
- Good at attracting interest to your study.

Disadvantages
- Need to be careful about how you define your target and study populations, since there may be common characteristics among those who participate, not reflected among those who do not.

e Self-administered questionnaire

The procedure here is to hand over a questionnaire with an explanation, and then call back later to collect it.

Advantages
- Saves time.
- Allows questions to be asked that might otherwise require a postal survey (ie sensitive questions or those requiring a considered response).

Disadvantages
- Any questions which are ambiguous or misunderstood may lead to incorrect or false data.

f Direct observation

Sometimes necessary because of the nature of the study, but can be time consuming and costly.

Choosing the right data collection method for your choice of sample design

We looked at a number of sample designs in Chapter 5, and found that certain sample designs suit particular data collection methods. For example, quota sampling would be difficult by post, since we do not know which sub-groups the subjects fall into and cannot monitor our quotas. Simple random sampling could not be applied to high street or mall interviews very easily, since we would not have a sampling frame to select from. Quota sampling or systematic sampling are often used in this sort of situation, where the subjects are on the move.

Non-response

Postal surveys can cut down on costs, but the level of non-response will be greater than, for example, with one-to-one interviews.

There are things you can do to minimise the levels of non-response. Below are some basic ideas that go a long way towards achieving this.

a Pre-notification of postal surveys

Before the questionnaire is sent in the post, a postcard is sent informing the subject that a questionnaire will be arriving and stressing the importance of the survey, etc. This seems to improve the response rate, perhaps by creating anticipation in the minds of the recipients.

b Follow-up enquiries

The evidence seems to be that postal surveys attain an initial response rate of less than 50 per cent. Follow up the non-responders with a letter. Then follow up any still missing with a telephone call or personal visit.

c Incentives or rewards

For example, highlighting the key benefits of the survey to them and you. Entry to free prize draws or the offer of free gifts can be used, but this depends on your budget!

There is another type of non-response, in which only part of the data is provided for some of the subjects in the sample. Asking sensitive questions on ethnic origin, political views, age, etc, in people surveys could lead to a number of non-responses on this or other questions. This will leave you with patchy data that could be difficult to analyse.

One way of improving this situation would be to allow respondents to write down their reply to sensitive questions and put it in a sealed envelope, so that you cannot see it. Allowing them to complete the entire questionnaire and put it inside a sealed envelope is also an option. If you are using quota sampling, though, you will need to record basic data to monitor your quotas.

Non-response is a problem in that there can often be some common characteristics among non-responders. As a result the sample you end up with could be biased and unrepresentative.

 Activity 7.1

For your survey, jot down any ideas or thoughts on the method of data collection that you propose to use. You may wish to consider ideas for improving the level of response. In addition, you may need to reconsider and perhaps alter slightly the thoughts and ideas you jotted down in Activity 6.2 relating to the sample design. (If so, go back to it now and make the necessary changes.) When you feel happy with the details for this activity and Activity 6.2, you can complete the sections relating to the survey design and data collection form in your survey plan (Remember, Appendix 4 has some examples of completed survey plans that may help.)

---

8 Pilot surveys

What is a pilot survey?

A pilot survey is a scaled-down version of the full survey. You simply:
- collect a small portion of the data;
- stop your survey;
- assess how it has gone;
- modify the full survey as required before undertaking it.

This is a good thing to do if you are not particularly experienced at designing sample surveys.

How can a pilot survey help?

A pilot survey can help with answering the following questions, which should be asked before the full survey is undertaken.

- Are all the subjects in the sample accessible and are we going to get the sort of sample we hoped for? In particular, are there subjects with certain common characteristics that look like being difficult to include in the sample? ie How do our target and study populations compare?
- Is the chosen sample design appropriate and practical?
- Are we conducting the survey in the most cost effective and efficient way? For example, are the arrangements for transport, post, personnel, etc, OK?
- Is the method of data collection the most appropriate? Are there any problems, ambiguities, etc with the questionnaire?
- Are our estimates of time and costs reasonable and can the survey be completed within the proposed time scales?
- Are we likely to obtain the right data in order to conduct the intended analyses?

How should a pilot survey be conducted?

The key points are that a pilot survey should not take too long to do, but should cover sufficient subjects in order to assess the sorts of issues we saw above.

Typically for a large-scale survey, having a sample size of some several thousand subjects taking several months to complete, a pilot survey covering a few hundred subjects over one or two weeks would be appropriate. A small-scale survey, having a sample size of 100 subjects taking one day to complete, would probably only need five subjects or so, taking about 30 minutes to do.

Activity 8.1

For your survey, jot down any ideas that you may have for a pilot survey. For example, how many subjects, how long it should take, which subjects, where it should take place and when. Then enter these details in your survey plan. (Remember the examples of completed survey plans in Appendix 4.)

If the completed pilot survey shows that there are no major changes required to the full survey, then there should be no problems with using the data from the pilot survey in the full survey. If, however, there are changes to the survey that mean the pilot data may be different to the full survey data in some way, then you must be careful about including the pilot data in your results.

9 Calculating the sample size

How big should your sample be?

This is a question that is probably often asked or thought of, but not answered very well. The reason is that few non-statistical specialists really understand the statistical theory required to answer it. Do you?

There are two ways to approach the question of determining the sample size, either by using theory or by considering the practicalities of various sample size possibilities. If you were really clever you would include both of these methods in your calculations.

a The theoretical approach

Essentially, the sample size is connected to the level of accuracy you desire in your results. The greater the level of accuracy, the bigger the sample size. The chapter on sample surveys in Anderson *et al.* (1993), gives a basic introduction to sample size calculations. Scheaffer *et al.* (1990) go into more detail.

b The practical approach

It is worth remembering that no matter how accurate your sample size calculations are, you should still balance the need for accuracy with the costs involved in using a sample that size. A common way of determining sample size is by including as many subjects in the survey as cost/time will allow. Another way is purely by gut feeling. For example, it may be obvious that only 10 subjects is not enough, but that 10,000 is totally unnecessary. You therefore need to find a number between these two figures that will provide enough information to give at least some validity to the results, but that is also within your time/budget constraints.

10 Closing remarks on undertaking your survey

Being able to consider all of the issues explored in this part, all at the same time, isn't easy. Indeed, even the so-called experts get it wrong. Remember the pre-election polls for the UK general election of 1992? (It turned out that a lot of people who would not take part in the poll declined to do so because at the time they did not wish to reveal that they planned to vote Conservative. This meant that the study population did not adequately represent the potential Conservative vote.)

All you can do is take some time to think and plan ahead. Getting someone else's opinion on questions you may ask could help. The time spent planning and thinking should easily be saved in not having to sort out the results from a badly run survey.

 Activity 10.1

The time that you take for this activity will depend on the size of your survey. When you feel ready:
- undertake your pilot survey;
- modify your survey plan in light of the outcome of your pilot survey;
- undertake the full survey.

Having completed the full survey, examine what the true study population has been, and enter the details of this in the survey plan. When reporting the conclusions of your survey, refer to the study population and not the target population.

---

11 Bibliography

The following is a list of some of the texts on survey sampling and related topics, referred to in this part.

Anderson, D. R. *et al.* (1993) *Statistics for business and economics*, New York, West Publishing.

Barnett, V. (1991) *Sample survey principles and methods*, London, Edward Arnold.

Belson, W. (1986) *Validity in survey research*, Aldershot, Gower.

Cochran, W. (1977) *Sampling techniques*, New York, Wiley.

Frey, J. (1989) *Survey research by telephone*, London, Sage.

Kish, L. (1965) *Survey sampling*, New York, Wiley.

Neave, H.R. (1978) *Statistics tables*, London, Allen & Unwin.

Raj, D. (1972) *The design of sample surveys*, New York, McGraw-Hill.

Scheaffer, R. L., Mendenhall, W. and Ott, L. (1990) *Elementary survey sampling*, Kent, PWS.

Appendix 1: Solutions

Solution to Activity 4.1

Survey example	Subject
C	*Person*
D	*Director*
E	*Customer*
F	*Customer*
G	*Police officer*
H	*Road*
I	*Person*
J	*Car*
K	*Student*

Solution to Activity 4.3

C The study population contains people who do not intend to vote, as well as those who do. The target population excluded those who did not intend to vote, since the intention was to predict the outcome of the election.

Therefore, the views of the sample could be different from the final vote, because it contains people who may well not vote.

K The study population consists only of students at the two universities mentioned, while the target population includes students at all universities and colleges throughout the UK. Since we cannot be sure that the students at these universities are representative of the whole of the UK, the results of the sample could not be applied to the target population.

Solution to Activity 4.5

D The sampling frame was a list of businesses in the business directory that was used to select from.

G This was a list of police officers on the employment records.

H This was a list of all the roads that cross the city boundary.

Solution to Activity 5.1

The random digits you should have selected from the table are in bold type below:

6583 6840 8940 3769 7791 3013 0692 8799 3226 2754 7754 2659
9221 4897 6545 1010 6072 3690 1993 6025 7233 1712 7195 8799
8224 6505 6369 0494 6656 8632 0847 6773 1076 5517 8597 8960
2739 4587 7841 5503 3727 7250 3572 5884 4750 8534 2584 7155
5060 **9674 1531 6736 5000 8978 73**53 1674 6942 5942 7333 7485

8058 2773 9048 5697 1201 8823 0481 9358 1273 4799 0127 6687
8300 3857 7677 0989 0496 3644 7653 2281 6355 8041 8868 1501
8099 1573 1638 2713 6569 4635 9050 2472 6627 9618 1979 1479
5471 9649 1129 1615 2885 5496 1253 9413 6651 0767 8149 4984
7302 0779 0088 6900 0974 7142 1058 3685 4541 3691 2484 3051

So that the books we select are: 96 74 15 31 67 36 50 00 89 78 73

Note that we have 11 random numbers here. This is because one of them, the 00, is useless.

Solution to Activity 5.2

$$\frac{\text{No. of sampling units}}{\text{Sample size}} = \frac{99}{10} = 9.9, \text{ ie } 10$$

Therefore, we need to choose our first customer from the first 10, and select every tenth customer from then on.

The four-digit number in row 20, column 10 is 1810, so our first two-digit random number would be 18, which is no good since it is not in the first 10. Our next random number is 10. Therefore we would select customer number 10 as our first to be interviewed. The full list of customers is therefore:

10 20 30 40 50 60 70 80 90 and 100!

We assume only 99 customers will visit, so perhaps instead of using customer 100, we could include customer 99.

Solution to Activity 5.3

The sample size in each of the 28 strata are as follows:

Age	Total	Male	Female
0–4	398	206	192
5–9	485	250	235
10–14	491	253	238
15–19	451	231	220
20–24	476	244	232
25–29	490	251	239
30–34	458	234	224
35–39	398	203	195
40–44	254	130	124
45–49	227	115	112
50–54	205	103	102
55–59	191	103	88
60–64	176	103	73
64+	298	158	140
Totals	**4,998**	**2,584**	**2,414**

Note that they do not add up exactly to 5,000. This is because of rounding. It doesn't really matter whether you have 5,000 or 4,998 in the sample!

Solution to Activity 5.4

	survey example
Simple randon sampling	F
Systematic sampling	E
Stratified sampling	D, G, H
Quota sampling	B, C, I
Cluster sampling	I
Judgemental sampling	
Convenience sampling	J, K

Appendix 2: Table of random digits

6583 6840 8940 3769 7791 3013 0692 8799 3226 2754 7754 2659
9221 4897 6545 1010 6072 3690 1993 6025 7233 1712 7195 8799
8224 6505 6369 0494 6656 8632 0847 6773 1076 5517 8597 8960
2739 4587 7841 5503 3727 7250 3572 5884 4750 8534 2584 7155
5060 9674 1531 6736 5000 8978 7353 1674 6942 5942 7333 7485

8058 2773 9048 5697 1201 8823 0481 9358 1273 4799 0127 6687
8300 3857 7677 0989 0496 3644 7653 2281 6355 8041 8868 1501
8099 1573 1638 2713 6569 4635 9050 2472 6627 9618 1979 1479
5471 9649 1129 1615 2885 5496 1253 9413 6651 0767 8149 4984
7302 0779 0088 6900 0974 7142 1058 3685 4541 3691 2484 3051

7347 8322 6063 9092 7714 3666 3508 5780 1895 0790 7323 4423
3081 5453 4170 2129 0968 0241 5352 4232 2771 8996 6001 3626
1482 5950 9171 4925 6965 7104 7053 4002 9964 4851 3318 5345
2202 8242 0447 8455 3094 5250 3482 0392 7741 0316 8547 9874
3798 5086 2347 9983 1426 3153 2471 9029 0101 9602 0868 3173

4564 1312 7787 5395 7853 7248 8839 4612 5585 2864 7443 8766
9846 4636 0492 3336 7402 2703 6236 6946 4434 1422 9960 1392
4044 1860 2662 0879 4923 7933 7265 2734 3607 4347 9100 4944
7436 2966 0376 5875 7881 5423 0287 2914 2052 8149 0505 8171
6198 2168 3854 1668 9094 5623 8431 2806 1330 1810 3953 4803

6006 2331 8846 4777 9444 9091 7479 0216 2846 2685 4405 9371
4465 8888 1824 8540 5765 4312 0438 5968 7159 2316 8162 4955
9045 8091 8472 8974 4714 9916 4432 4014 4343 8797 9975 4976
8843 5462 4044 2474 4658 0334 3620 0326 4003 0749 2765 0659
8033 7617 9514 6012 9705 9703 1599 1169 1844 5914 9492 1221

2561 4981 2918 5241 9447 6159 2365 3412 3747 6408 1271 2035
3248 5131 2812 0770 9874 4531 3588 4974 4105 6029 1323 5747
1766 7186 6148 7945 8029 4693 4500 6463 4975 1488 4944 0951
2342 3592 2447 0107 1728 2012 4541 4865 7335 5690 7396 1726
9479 1408 9401 2910 1870 3074 5283 3098 9578 7602 9990 8370

5461 7028 3684 8559 2169 3943 7490 9627 3151 3364 8342 2965
6793 5840 6585 6634 2075 1036 5991 4813 0577 0119 1337 9246
9624 0008 4366 2250 9261 2009 6825 2222 5104 0729 6419 9021
0168 1295 2689 3083 3241 4200 4260 4729 4411 2855 2341 8623
8915 9164 0548 5154 9385 9864 3084 8799 7179 9705 3821 1329

2594 3396 6798 6087 2551 5902 3459 8077 4826 6421 7403 7067
4429 8444 3266 7339 0680 9222 2893 7456 0093 8742 5182 1871
6994 9607 7252 5866 9649 1175 0266 1606 1105 1024 3834 4839
2657 8888 6847 2718 4880 4173 7927 7733 0968 6066 1543 8770
1292 5464 5718 6370 1432 1919 1898 3299 9466 7460 9120 0862

Produced using MINITAB.

Appendix 3: Example of a tally sheet used for the foot measurement survey

Male/age tally sheet

Age	Tally	Sheet total	Grand total	Target	Grand total target
0–4					
5–9					
10–14					
15–19					
20–24					
25–29					
30–34					
35–39					
40–44					
45–49					
50–54					
55–59					
60–64					
64+					
Total					

Appendix 4: Examples of completed survey plans

Eg Example 1: Library loan survey

Survey plan

Survey title: University library loan survey.

Aims of survey
To assess how often books are taken out of the library, by establishing the number of times each book was loaned over the previous academic year. In addition comparisons of lending rates between various degree courses will be examined.

Location(s) of survey: College/university library.

Population details

Subject: Individual books.

Sampling unit (if different): Same.

Target population: All books in the library, including short-loan, seven-day loan etc, but excluding the reference collection, periodicals, abstracts, theses, etc.

Study population (to be completed after survey has been conducted):

Type of sample design to be used: simple random sampling.

Details of sampling frame (including details of any deficiencies with the frame): Library's inventory of book stock as at 1 July 1994 will be used as a list from which to select books.

Details of how subjects are to be selected (including details of how subjects that are difficult to access will be included):
The 1,000 short-loan books will be numbered from 1 to 1,000, while the 8,000 others will be numbered 1,001 to 9,000. Random numbers in the range 1 to 9,999 will be generated using the statistical package MINITAB. Any random numbers above 9,000 will be discarded, and the others used to select books from the sampling frame. It is not envisaged that the information on any selected book will be too difficult to obtain.

Sample size (also give sub-group sizes etc): 500 books in total.

Data collection method(s) to be employed (including details of forms, verbal questions to be used, instructions to personnel):
A data collection form will be used to enter the information for each chosen book from the library's records. This will be undertaken by Fred Bloggs.

Pilot survey:

Total number of subjects (also state how this is broken down into sub-groups if appropriate): 10 books. No sub-groups.

Characteristics of subjects to be included in pilot survey: Nothing particularly, just use first books chosen at random.

Time scale for conducting pilot survey: To take place as soon as is practical, taking possibly about 30 minutes to complete.

Location of pilot survey: University library.

Details of data to be collected and data analysis to be performed:
The variables to be recorded are as given on the data collection form. In particular,

the number of times the book has been loaned during the previous academic year is the primary variable.

The data are to be stored in a spreadsheet using SuperCalc or Lotus 1-2-3. Once entered, the data will be checked manually against the original data collection form.

Comparisons in loan rates between degree courses will be undertaken using the statistical technique analysis of variance (one way), with degree course as the factor of interest. All tests will be done at the 5 per cent level and two sailed hypothesis tests will be used throughout. The statistics package MINITAB will be used for all analyses.

Example 2: Foot measurement survey

Survey plan

Survey title: Anthropometric survey of Taiwan.

Aims of survey
To obtain information on the foot dimensions of the population of the country, in order to produce a number of foot lasts (wooden moulds or models) that can be used to manufacture shoes which will fit a reasonable proportion of the population.

Location(s) of survey: Districts 2, 4 and 7 of Taiwan.

Population details
    Subject: Residents of Taiwan.

    Sampling unit (if different): Same.

    Target population: All residents.

    Study population (to be completed after survey has been conducted):

Type of sample design to be used: a quota sample will be taken in districts 2, 4 and 7.

Details of sampling frame (including details of any deficiencies with the frame): Not applicable since quota sampling is being used.

Details of how subjects are to be selected (including details of how subjects that are difficult to access will be included):
The subjects are to be classified by age, sex and district. The overall sample size will be allocated using equal allocation (the sub-group sample size calculations should be given in an attached document). The subjects will be measured at places of employment (factories, offices, etc), at home, at school/college, etc, until sufficient

numbers have been obtained in each sub-group. Progress towards achieving these quotas will be monitored using tally sheets (these should be attached).

Sample size (also give sub-group sizes, etc): 10,000 feet in total.

Data collection method(s) to be employed (including details of forms, verbal questions to be used, instructions to personnel):
The subject's left foot will be washed and dried. One member of the measuring team will measure the foot, the other will record the data as it is called out. There will be a measuring team in each district working at the same time.

Pilot survey:

> **Total number of subjects** (also state how this is broken down into sub-groups if appropriate): 500 subjects in district 1. To include both sexes, but not necessarily any particular age groups. Also likely that subjects will be of only one or two areas of employment.

> **Characteristics of subjects to be included in pilot survey**: The subjects will only come from district 1.

> **Time scale for conducting pilot survey**: To take place during the first two weeks in July. The pilot is likely to take this amount of time to complete.

> **Location of pilot survey**: District 1.

Details of data to be collected and data analysis to be performed:
The variables to be recorded are as given on the data collection form.

The data are to be stored in a spreadsheet using SuperCalc or Lotus 1-2-3. Once entered, the data will be checked manually against the original data collection form.

The foot measurements will be analysed using principal components analysis to establish the relationships between the various foot dimensions and to establish a range of fitting indices. The statistics package SAS will be used for this analysis.

Survey plan

Survey title:

Aims of survey:

Location(s) of survey:

Population details:

Subject:

Target population:

Study population (to be completed after survey has been conducted):

Sampling unit (if different):

Type of sample design to be used:

Details of sampling frame (including details of any deficiencies with the frame):

Details of how subjects are to be selected (including details of how subjects that are difficult to access will be included):

Sample size (also give sub-group sizes etc.):

Data collection method(s) to be employed (including details of forms, verbal questions to be used, instructions to personnel):

Pilot survey:

Total number of subjects (also state how this is broken down into sub-groups if appropriate):

Characteristics of subjects to be included in pilot survey:

Time scale for conducting pilot survey:

Location of pilot survey:

Details of data to be collected and data analysis to be performed:

Comments following completion of survey (give details on level of non-response, activities taken to follow up the non-responders, quality of data, subjects who/which were difficult to access, any discrepancies between target and study population, etc.)

Survey examples

A College/university library loan survey

Aim: To assess how often books are taken out of the college/university library, by establishing the number of times each book is loaned over the previous academic year.

Target population: All books in the library, including short-loan, seven-day loan, etc, but excluding reference collection, periodicals, abstracts, theses, etc.

Approach to sampling: This example will be used extensively in our discussions, with a number of different approaches to sampling. To make it simpler, we will initially assume that there are 8,000 normal-loan books and 1,000 books for short-loan/seven-day loan (there may be actually quite a few more than this!).

B Poll of voting intentions conducted prior to general election

Aim: To establish voting intentions of those eligible to vote and intending to vote, in order to forecast the outcome of the election.

Target population: Those eligible to vote and who intend to turn out on the day of the election to vote.

Approach to sampling: The target population, usually identified by the most recent national census, is subdivided into various groups, for example by age and sex and perhaps by other factors such as area of the UK (Scotland, North-West England, etc). This would give sub-groups such as males aged 18 to 29, 30 to 39, etc and females aged 18 to 29, 30 to 39, etc, in each area.

The proportions in each of these sub-groups making up the target population are to be reflected in the sample. This is achieved by visiting appropriate types of households in various areas until these proportions are at least approximately achieved.

Each person interviewed is also asked whether or not they intend to turn out and vote. Anyone stating that they do not intend to vote is not included in the sample used to predict the outcome of the election.

C Poll of voting intentions conducted prior to general election

(As **B** above with slight modification)

Aim: Same as for **B**.

Target population: Same as for **B**.

Approach to sampling: Same as for **B**.

Modification: Each person interviewed is not asked whether or not they intend to turn out to vote. Therefore the sample will include those who do not intend voting.

D Survey of business confidence

Aim: To establish the views of managing directors of companies from various sectors of industry (in a particular city), regarding confidence in the recovery of the economy. In particular, to make comparisons between the various industrial sectors.

Target population: All businesses in the area under study.

Approach to sampling: Those businesses listed in a particular business directory are divided into various types (manufacturing, financial, leisure, etc). Businesses are selected at random from the directory and contacted by telephone, until the proportions of each type of business reflect the proportions in the directory. The telephone contact is to establish whether or not the managing director is willing for the company to take part in the survey. Those saying no are discarded from the sample, whereas those agreeing are sent a questionnaire.

E Customer profile survey

Aim: A particular chain of stationery shops wishes to establish the views of its customers, in order to develop its business appropriately, improve sales and so on.

Target population: All customers using the shops.

Approach to sampling: Every tenth customer (or whatever interval is appropriate to establish required sample size), is interviewed on leaving the store, irrespective of whether or not they have made a purchase. If a customer declines to take part, every following customer is asked until one finally agrees.

F Customer profile survey

(As **E** with slight modification)

Aim: Same as for **E**.

Target population: Same as for **E**.

Modification is in the approach to sampling: Customers are counted as they leave the shop and each is given a sequential reference number, eg 1, 2, 3. This is done so that those customers whose reference numbers match a list of numbers that were generated at random are interviewed. Again this is done irrespective of whether or not they have made a purchase. If a customer declines to take part, each customer which follows is asked until one finally agrees.

G Survey of stress levels experienced by police officers in a particular county

Aim: To establish a means of measuring the levels of stress being experienced by police officers, and assess whether or not there are any significant factors influencing the amount of stress they experience. Of particular interest are any significant differences between males and females and between the various ranks from Constable upwards.

Target population: All police officers up to and including the rank of Inspector.

Approach to sampling: A sample of officers to include male and female, Constables, Sergeants and Inspectors, are selected at random from personnel records, such that the proportions in each of the above sub-groups employed in the county are reflected in the same way in the sample.

H Survey of daily levels of traffic flow across a city boundary

Aim: To establish the numbers of cars, buses, lorries, and so on, flowing into and out of the city boundary on all roads each day. This is part of an exercise assessing the impact of traffic levels on the environment.

Target population: All roads that carry traffic across the city boundary.

Approach to sampling: Using County Hall records of all the roads that cross the city boundary, the roads are sub-grouped according to the class of road (A road, B road, etc) and their postal districts. A number of roads from each sub-group are then selected at random from the lists. These selected roads have their traffic flow measured at various strategic points, inside and outside the city boundary.

I Anthropometric (foot measurement) survey of a country

Aim: To obtain information on the foot dimensions of the population of the country, in order to produce a number of foot lasts (wooden moulds or models) that can be used to manufacture shoes which will fit a reasonable proportion of the population.

Target population: All inhabitants of the country.

Approach to sampling: Using information obtained from the most recent census, the population is divided into sub-groups according to age and sex. In addition, the country is divided into a number of areas (eg counties), and a number of areas selected at random. Within these areas, people are measured at work, at home, at school, etc, so that the number of subjects in each sub-group in the sample is in the same proportions as the whole population of the country.

J Reliability survey of used two-year-old cars

Aim: To establish the reliability of new cars during their first two years of life.

Target population: All cars on UK roads with a certain registration prefix (eg K).

Approach to sampling: Viewers of a certain motoring magazine programme and readers of an associated monthly publication are invited to take part in the survey if they own a car registered with that prefix.

K Survey into the financial state of students

Aim: To assess the position regarding student finances across the UK, and to make comparisons between the different parts of the country, between males and females and between the various categories of student (undergraduate, mature undergraduate, postgraduate, etc).

Target population: *All* students at all universities and colleges throughout the UK.

Approach to sampling: Students at your own university/college together with another local and similar institution are interviewed as they pass certain locations around the respective campuses.

Part C: Questionnaire design

Introduction

This part aims to equip you to plan, design and distribute a questionnaire. It assumes you have reviewed various ways of collecting data and have chosen to issue a questionnaire after considering the alternatives. Among the advantages of questionnaires are accuracy, access to dispersed respondents and wide coverage in terms of topics and respondents. The possible disadvantages are the expense, some delay in getting results, and in some cases potential for disruption or arousing false hopes among respondents. There is also the need for some expertise in designing and processing a questionnaire properly – but then, you are taking care of that by studying these chapters!

This part takes you through to the point of having received the replies. Although it does not tell you how to analyse the data, it does try to help you to generate *raw data* (data as it is first collected) in a form that will be easy to process and analyse.

Objectives

When you have completed the exercises in this part you should be able to:
- plan the design and distribution of a questionnaire within a realistic time scale, allowing for legal requirements;
- lay out the questionnaire in a way that is pleasing to the eye and makes it easy for the respondent to fill in and for you to analyse;
- write appropriate introductory material and concluding remarks;
- select the most appropriate forms of question (or forms of *item*, to use the correct term) for each part of a questionnaire requiring a response;
- avoid the most common errors in question design;
- arrange the questions in a sequence that facilitates response;
- write an appropriate covering letter;
- choose methods of distribution, collection and follow-up that minimise the risk of a biased sample.

Complete the activities in each section.

Notes on terminology

a The word *item* is used in preference to *question* because the request for information is often not phrased as a question.

b The word *population* is used to refer to the collection of things about which you are gathering information. Of course, the population is often made up of people, your respondents, but sometimes questionnaires gather information, not about people, but about companies, institutions, courses, publications, or a wide range of other things which then are referred to as the *population*.

12 Planning and logistics of questionnaire design

Quantitative or qualitative?

If your aim is to express your findings in figures, then you are planning a *quantitative* study. If, on the other hand, you are simply exploring to see what factors are involved in order to gain an understanding of a topic, without needing to know how often these factors occur, then you are making a *qualitative* study.

Qualitative research is sometimes sufficient to give all the information needed, eg in studying careers through a collection of case studies or in describing how a change was brought about in industrial relations, an interesting and convincing study might be made without any laborious numerical analysis.

Frequently, however, qualitative research is done as a preliminary step towards quantitative data. For example, a qualitative questionnaire could be used to identify important topics to provide the basis of a quantitative questionnaire.

Undoubtedly the great majority of questionnaires are designed with quantitative analysis in mind, though most contain a few items for qualitative analysis. Qualitative research usually uses other methods of data collection, such as interviews and observation.

Quantitative data are often gathered using items offering a choice of predetermined responses for easy analysis, whereas the nature of qualitative research prevents prediction of the categories into which the data can be placed for analysis. Thus qualitative data, while avoiding the complexities of statistical analysis, is much more time consuming to analyse.

 Activity 12.1

Let's check whether you are clear as to the relative merits of quantitative and qualitative studies. (The solutions are on page 99.)

    a A researcher is making an initial investigation to identify important factors or variables involved in gaining an understanding of the motivation provided by company cars. Which type of research is appropriate, quantitative or qualitative?

    b Which type is often done as a preliminary to the other type?

    c True or false? Quantitative data are usually analysed more quickly than qualitative data.

d Writing in answers in the respondent's own words, rather than ticking boxes, is typical of which kind of survey?

e Finally, just in case you are one of the many students who have trouble with the spelling of these two words, fill in the missing letters.

- Qual...................
- Quant..................

Legal requirements: the Data Protection Act

Before going further into the design of your questionnaire you should consider how you will analyse it. Great advantages can be gained by using a computer to analyse quantitative data, but serious constraints on this are laid down in the Data Protection Act. The essential requirement of the act is that, before you keep information regarding an individual in a form that permits it to be processed on a computer, you should register your specific intentions with the Office of the Data Protection Registrar, paying a fee of £75 to cover a three-year period. The restriction applies only to information on persons, not, for example, on companies.

It makes no difference whether your respondents agree to your use of the data. Nor is it enough to omit their names from your electronic record if data could be identified with a particular individual either from the same record or in conjunction with information the user (ie you) already possesses.

There are certain circumstances in which exemption from the Act is granted, but these are very restricted and do not apply to most questionnaires that students might wish to process on a computer. Although it would appear that the act is often disregarded by students and others, its application is being tightened and breach of it is a criminal act.

Clearly it is impossible to provide here detailed guidance to this complex law, but the office responsible provides full information to enquirers over the telephone and through publications, including a student pack. For information contact: The Office of the Data Protection Registrar, Springfield House, Water Lane, Wilmslow, Cheshire SK9 5AX. Enquiry helpline: 01625 535777.

Confidentiality and anonymity

People are more likely to be frank, especially on sensitive issues such as their views on their bosses, if they can remain anonymous. If they are requested to give their names but offered confidentiality regarding their individual replies, this requires a level of trust from respondents which it may not always be reasonable to expect.

When making arrangements so that responses cannot be traced to individuals (ie to provide anonymity), you need somehow to provide a way of knowing who has responded and who has not so you can make a selective follow-up.

One way of doing this is to provide each respondent with a blank envelope in which to seal the completed questionnaire and an additional slip of paper bearing his/her name. The respondent places both of these in an outer envelope and sends it to some trusted intermediary who then:

- opens the outer envelope;
- checks off the name on the slip of paper against the list of recipients of the questionnaire to show that a reply has been received and a follow-up is unnecessary;
- puts the sealed envelope containing the questionnaire in a box with the others already received, thus removing any connection with the respondent's name.

You may find that you are able to act as the trusted intermediary, or you may be able to enlist the help of a manager, trade union official, or even a consultant. Some large organisations use the Electoral Reform Society for this purpose.

Sample size

'How big does my sample have to be?'

This is a question everyone designing a questionnaire must ask themselves. The answer is critical if you are making a quantitative study, less important if your investigation is qualitative.

Determining the necessary sample size for a quantitative study is quite a complex matter. Any good textbook on research methods will have a section on this topic, eg Sekaran (1992) (see Chapter 19).

Sample size depends heavily on what *margin of error* you are willing to risk, that is, to what extent you can risk your sample being different from the whole population sampled. To give you an idea, a sample size of about 400 would be needed for you to be confident that 45 per cent to 55 per cent of your respondents held a certain view when your survey showed that 50 per cent of your sample held it. Thus quantitative data is expensive to collect with a reasonable degree of confidence.

On the other hand, in a qualitative study the sample need be only large enough to ensure a wide variety of answers. Indeed, it is unlikely to be very large as the task of analysing qualitative data (not fitted into predetermined slots) would be too great. In this case 20 or 30 replies might be enough.

Volunteer respondents

If your respondents are only those who felt like responding, ie are volunteers, then they may well be different in important respects from those who chose not to answer, so you cannot confidently state that a certain percentage of your whole target population has this or that characteristic. That is why a follow-up is needed to bring in enough of these reluctant respondents to ensure that your sample is representative of the whole population whose views you want.

Even when you are doing a qualitative study you need to be wary of having only volunteer respondents. For example, if you were examining opinions regarding a particular library service, it would not be enough to gather only the views of those who chose to answer a questionnaire voluntarily taken from a pile left at the issue desk, as this might omit people in a hurry, perhaps due to slow service in the library.

Identifying subject areas

When asking questions about a person's attitudes with regard to a certain object, you usually have some potential subject areas in mind. For example, if you are trying to determine the training needs of office managers, you might suspect that they want training in human relations and in office procedures (filing, security, telephone skills, etc). If you have already found published material that points out these areas, then you may be able to ask specific questions in each area based on what previous researchers had discovered.

On the other hand, if you are starting from scratch to identify the important areas in a particular field, you may need to do exploratory research before deciding what questions to ask. While a questionnaire with numerous open questions (see Chapter 14, pages 82–86) can be useful for this purpose, sometimes a better alternative is to arrange unstructured interviews with a few typical respondents in order to see which topics emerge.

Determining appropriate length

People often ask 'How long can a questionnaire be?' This clearly depends on the type of respondent. A poorly educated shopfloor worker may find it tiring to answer only ten items, whereas a verbally skilled academic might answer 30 in the same time with less effort.

In any case, there is no point in including unnecessary questions. One way of avoiding unnecessary items is to *plan in advance how you are going to analyse the data*. Of course, this is possible only with responses chosen from predetermined alternatives (closed questions). Outline the exhibits (tables and figures) you expect to use in your report, without the actual values, then devise questions to provide the raw data to be analysed in order to produce the desired exhibits.

73

The number of potential exhibits easily produced by computer with modern statistics packages often surprises researchers. Suppose you ask respondents five questions about themselves (eg age, sex, level of management, length of service, etc) and then ten questions about their opinions. You thus have potentially 50 tables or figures produced by cross tabulation, when each of the ten opinion items is analysed five ways in terms of age, sex, etc, even without counting analyses into whether certain kinds of opinion go together. Clearly, it is better to keep the number of items low and concentrate on certain issues.

Another constraint on the length of the questionnaire is the need not to make it so long as to deter the respondent from starting it. Depending on the motivation of the respondent, a questionnaire can require up to about ten minutes to complete. Longer than that would seem to risk causing respondents to put off filling it in until they have more time. You can check completion time required during piloting, subtracting time taken discussing problems with your respondents.

Typical time scale

Designing a questionnaire involves various stages, which are shown below with the typical time required under the usual student conditions.

a Identify topic areas and develop initial items .... 1 week

b Discuss with tutor and revise .... 1 week

c Try out (*pilot*) and revise .... 1 week

d Print questionnaire and mail .... 1 week

e Wait before first follow-up .... 2 weeks

f Wait for follow-up responses .... 1 week

g Key in and analyse data .... 2 weeks

Total .... **9 weeks**

Obviously these figures can vary considerably according to the proportion of the student's time available for the project. They assume:
- that facilities are available;
- that only one follow-up is required to bring in enough replies from those who did not respond to your first request;
- that the persons needed for discussion and piloting are available without delay. (Piloting is discussed in more detail in Chapter 17.)

Note, too, that this total does not include the time needed to register with the Office of the Data Protection Registrar if necessary, nor writing up in report form, only processing of the data to provide a basis for discussion and recommendations.

Main components of questionnaires

Most questionnaires are made up of the following parts:

a **A title**.

b **A case number** uniquely identifying each completed questionnaire. This number is usually written by the researcher in a box marked *For office use only* in the top right corner of the first page upon receipt of the filled-in questionnaire, starting at 1.

c **Introductory remarks**. If there is no covering letter these will include the usual contents of such a letter (see Chapter 16). With or without a covering letter the questionnaire itself should provide the necessary assurances regarding confidentiality or anonymity as the case may be.

d **Instructions for completing items**. Unless these are self-evident, they are given just before the first items requiring a new mode of completion (circling numbers, ticking boxes, etc).

e **Respondent data**. These cover such matters as name, age, job title, grade, level of management, sex, salary, years of service, etc. Usually it is not the primary purpose of the questionnaire to gather such data; rather, they permit the focal data, eg opinions or attitudes, to be analysed in terms of the kinds of people who hold these views. Thus attitudes to taxes on petrol and diesel might be analysed in terms of those who own cars and those who do not.

f **Focal data**. These items gather data on the attitudes or opinions that lie at the core of your enquiry.

g **Open questions** to capture topics that might otherwise have escaped notice. These are covered in more detail in Chapter 14, page 82.

h **Closing remarks**. You should always thank your respondent and indicate here how to get the completed questionnaire back to you.

Note: the respondent data and focal data need not necessarily refer to people and opinions. For example, your respondents might be universities and the focal data might be the kinds of counselling and support services they offer.

13 Layout

Introductory remarks

It is helpful to give the questionnaire a heading, if only for your own convenience, for example in the follow-up. Don't repeat explanations given in the covering letter, except for those regarding confidentiality or anonymity. However, if there is no covering letter then briefly explain the reason for the survey.

All the instructions needed to complete and return the questionnaire should be on the questionnaire itself rather than in the covering letter; this is in case the two become separated. Instructions for completing the first item should be given (eg *Please tick appropriate box, Please circle number closest to your views*, etc). When the method of responding changes, give new instructions.

When an item may not be applicable to the respondent (for example, satisfaction with the car hired on holiday, when they did not hire one), allow for this possibility in your instructions, asking the respondent to skip any items which do not apply.

Sequence and grouping of items

 Activity 13.1

It may seem to you that the best order for the various parts of a questionnaire is pretty obvious, so see if you already know how to do this by arranging the following in the most suitable order within a typical questionnaire.
a   Position of respondent in organisation.
b   Open questions to capture matters overlooked in the other items.
c   Sensitive questions on income.
d   Name (if respondent wishes to give it).
e   Instructions for sending completed questionnaire to researcher.
f   Assurances on confidentiality.
g   Case number (serial number of completed questionnaire).

Activity 13.1 – solution

Several requirements need to be met in deciding on the order of items.

- The first few items should be easy to answer, to encourage the respondent to start writing. For example, you would not begin by asking questions on such sensitive matters as income or sexual orientation.

- Nor would such items be left to the very end. They are usually best placed less conspicuously in the middle of your questionnaire.

- Items requiring similar modes of response, such as ticking boxes, circling numbers, ranking options, or crossing out inapplicable terms, should be grouped so the respondent's concentration is not disrupted by constantly having to adapt to a new form of response.

- The open questions used to capture overlooked aspects are best left to the end. When respondents are invited to give name and address for further contact, this can conveniently be left to the end too.

- Assurances regarding anonymity or confidentiality need to be given early so as to encourage a response; thus the place for them is in the covering letter and in the introductory remarks on the questionnaire proper.

In the light of these points, the most likely appropriate order of the parts listed would be: f, g, a, c, b, d, e (g may come before f).

Numbering of items

The numbering of responses is often made unnecessarily complex. The simple rule is *number every response in a single series*.

This means that rather than having section A, B, etc and items B1, B2, etc, the responses will be numbered 1, 2, 3, etc from the beginning of the survey. Any necessary grouping can easily be done by the computer later at the analysis stage. The convenience of this simple numbering will become apparent in the discussion below on coding.

A convenient place for item numbers is at the left margin. If you give number 1 to the case number box described earlier, which you fill in, the *respondent's* first entry will be for item 2. This causes less puzzlement if the number is detached a little from the question by placing it at the extreme left margin. There follows an example of items 12 to 16 from a questionnaire.

How important to you are the following? (Please tick box)			
	Very imp.	Rather imp.	Not imp.
12 Good pay	☐ 1	☐ 2	☐ 3
13 Interesting work	☐ 1	☐ 2	☐ 3
14 Job security	☐ 1	☐ 2	☐ 3

15 How long have you been a sales supervisor?

0–2 years ☐ ¹

3–5 years ☐ ²

6–9 years ☐ ³

10 or more ☐ ⁴

16 Have you ever worked overseas? ☐ ¹ Yes ☐ ⁰ No

Note that the question introducing a series of items (12 to 14 above) is not itself numbered.

Coding for computer input

Computers work best with numbers, so responses are coded numerically for ease of entry and analysis. For example, instead of entering the word *No*, a zero (*0*) can be entered, *1* being entered for *Yes*.

It saves time and effort to pre-code the responses, rather than write in the codes on each completed questionnaire afterwards. Only when you cannot pre-determine the answers, ie in the case of open questions, is it necessary later to add codes corresponding to the categories you have chosen in the light of the range of responses received.

Some respondents feel put off by a mass of coding numbers, so it is best to keep these unobtrusive unless the respondent is actually expected to choose the number itself, eg by circling it.

Avoid forcing the respondent to memorise your codes. Thus, instead of saying only: *'Please enter a number from 1 (poor) to 5 (excellent) corresponding to your assessment of each aspect below'*, include the numbers from 1 to 5 for each item in the columns headed *Poor…Excellent*.

It helps keying the responses into a computer if the marked codes for the responses are towards the right hand side of the paper, perhaps even in a column at the right if the alignment with the item can be made quite clear.

Also, be sure that the boxes are close to the words they apply to. For example, the arrangement below could lead to incorrect replies:

Male ☐   Female ☐

The following activity will give you some experience of numbering and coding items.

Activity 13.2

Add the necessary numbers for item numbering and coding to the extract from a questionnaire given below.

Please circle the number for each response that most closely corresponds to your view.

	Agree strongly	Tend to agree	Tend to disagree	Disagree strongly
A person driving an expensive car is probably important.				
I get a lot of satisfaction from getting away at the lights faster than others.				
I would feel uncomfortable if I had to drive a low-powered car.				
I notice the model numbers on the back of cars ahead of me.				
I notice the registration letter of cars ahead of me.				
I dislike women driving fast cars.				

Does your present car have a sunroof?　　Yes　　No

If the answer to the previous question is **Yes** please answer the following two questions: Otherwise go to Q. ...

How often do you use the sunroof?

	Nearly always	75% of the time	50% of the time	25% of the time	Hardly ever
When it is sunny					
When it is warm					

How important to you are the following features of your car?

	Very important	Rather important	Not very important	Not at all important
Latest model				
Sporty look				
Expensive				
Good mileage per gallon				

Activity 13.2 – solution

	Agree strongly	Tend to agree	Tend to disagree	Disagree strongly
1 A person driving an expensive car is probably important.	1	2	3	4
2 I get a lot of satisfaction from getting away at the lights faster than others.	1	2	3	4
3 I would feel uncomfortable if I had to drive a low-powered car.	1	2	3	4
4 I notice the model numbers on the back of cars ahead of me.	1	2	3	4
5 I notice the registration letter of cars ahead of me.	1	2	3	4
6 I dislike women driving fast cars.	1	2	3	4

7 Does your present car have a sunroof?   Yes 1   No 0

If the answer to the previous question is **Yes**
please answer the following two questions: Otherwise go to Q.10

How often do you use the sunroof?

		Nearly always	75% of the time	50% of the time	25% of the time	Hardly ever
8	When it is sunny	1	2	3	4	5
9	When it is warm	1	2	3	4	5

How important to you are the following features of your car?

		Very important	Rather important	Not very important	Not at all important
10	Latest model	1	2	3	4
11	Sporty look	1	2	3	4
12	Expensive	1	2	3	4
13	Good mileage per gallon	1	2	3	4

Note: Did you remember to number each response, but only responses? If you did, congratulations. Some people find this activity hard.

Closing remarks

The concluding items are usually open questions, for the reasons given in Chapter 14, page 82. If you are inviting respondents to give their names for possible follow-up interviews or clarification of doubts, do this at the end. Finally, thank them for their help and explain how they should return the completed questionnaire.

 Activity 13.3

Now for a review quiz on layout and terminology. (The solutions are on page 99.)

a What is the name of the unique identifying number given to each completed questionnaire upon receipt?

b What is the correct term to apply to each passage in a questionnaire requiring a response?

c True or false? When the questionnaire is not anonymous it is a good idea to ask respondents to begin by entering their names (and addresses if needed) in order to get them started with something easy to answer.

d True or false? It is best to leave sensitive or highly personal questions until just before the end of the questionnaire so as not to put the respondents off answering.

e True or false? Items requiring the same mode of response (ticking, circling numbers, etc) should be grouped together whenever possible.

f True or false? Identifying items by numbers within sections (eg C1, C2 within section C) is more logical, making analysis easier.

g True or false? The boxes, etc for response should be placed directly under the statements to which they apply.

h True or false? Item numbers should be placed in the extreme right margin to facilitate computer processing.

i What sort of items are usually placed before the closing remarks?

---

14 Forms of item

Open and closed questions

It is useful to distinguish between open and closed questions in questionnaire design and other data-gathering situations.

A *closed question* is one where the possible responses are predetermined, typically the kind that ask the respondent to tick boxes, circle numbers, etc. For example:

Have you ever been appraised by your supervisor?
   Yes *(1)*
   No *(0)*

or

Means of travel to work
   Car   *(1)*
   Bus   *(2)*
   Bicycle *(3)*
   Other *(4)*

In contrast, an *open question* (eg *What did you like most about the course?*) has a large number of possible answers. Because the response to an open question is unpredictable, a generous space should be provided for the respondent to write it in. Open questions have the advantages of capturing ideas not thought of by the researcher and of allowing respondents to express their views when they may have had no previous opportunity to do so.

On the other hand, responses to open questions are obviously more difficult to analyse as the analysis cannot be planned in advance. Another disadvantage of open questions is that they slow down answering by causing respondents to search their memory in order to recall, rather than simply recognise, the responses. Indeed, respondents may be discouraged from answering open questions if they are uncertain what to say or have a poor command of language.

For this reason, and to act as items to pick up interesting points not covered in closed questions, open questions are best placed towards the end of the questionnaire.

Dichotomous items

Items which offer only two alternatives are called *dichotomous* items. Examples are *Yes/No* questions, or *Agree/Disagree* items. When you are assessing something that can exist to varying degrees, you get more information if you measure how much is present, rather than just whether any is present or not.

For example, instead of asking:

Have you ever been to France?

Yes	*(1)*
No	*(0)*

you could ask:

How much time have you spent in France?

No time	*(1)*
Less than one week	*(2)*
1 to 2 weeks	*(3)*
3 to 6 weeks	*(4)*
More than 6 weeks	*(5)*

You would thus distinguish between a student who had spent a term on placement with a French firm and someone who has made only a day trip to Calais, both of whom would have answered *Yes* to the first item. Bear in mind that your analysis should also make use of the additional information provided by a graduated response as shown in the second item above.

Scaled items

Perhaps the most useful and widely used form of item is one where the respondent chooses a point on a scale which best represents his/her view. Scales with wording at various points along their length are known as a *Likert scales* after the prominent American management researcher who used them extensively (Likert, 1961).

For example:

a *A glass of wine a day will eventually damage the liver.*

Agree strongly	Tend to agree	Tend to disagree	Disagree strongly
1	2	3	4

There are other ways of showing how much the statement matches the respondent's attitude, such as:

b *At departmental meetings I feel bored.*

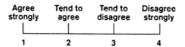

Nearly always	Often	Seldom	Hardly ever
1	2	3	4

c *How likely are you to enrol for a PhD?*

Very likely	Likely	Unlikely	Very unlikely
1	2	3	4

Another scaled form of response is *semantic differential*. It differs from the Likert scale in that there are words only at each end of the scale, not at different points along its length.

For example:
Describe your best male friend on the scales below by circling the number that most closely corresponds to him.

Stingy	1 2 3 4 5 6 7	Generous
Likes going to parties	1 2 3 4 5 6 7	Hates going to parties

Note that the ends of each *dimension* (as each item in a semantic differential scale is called) need not be marked with a single word; a phrase or even a sentence can be used. Semantic differential scales are easy for respondents to understand. The number of points on the scale is usually between five and ten. Research on semantic differential has shown that the most common dimensions to emerge are:

- bad–good,
- strong–weak,
- active–passive.

You may consider this when developing dimensions to describe a particular object of an attitude. There is no need to use these exact words, but derivatives of these three concepts may prove fruitful or interesting.

Mid-point or no mid-point?

You may have noticed that in the examples of scaled items above some had an even number of options, with no mid-point, while others had a mid-point. In fact, both semantic differential and Likert scales may have an odd or an even number of alternatives.

The mid-point of a dimension may sometimes be regarded by researchers as corresponding to a *don't care* answer, so they use items with no mid-point to lead respondents to express an opinion rather than taking the easy way out by going down the middle.

However, this is not always desirable, particularly when you are measuring a person's factual knowledge regarding some issue. For example, it is easy to imagine an item regarding nuclear power to which the most accurate answer for many people would be *don't know*. In this case, it would be better to provide a separate *don't know* option.

Moreover, some observant or knowledgeable respondents might resent being forced to express a view and this resentment might lead them to give reckless and thus probably inaccurate answers. So consider these factors when deciding whether to provide a mid-point or not. One solution is to provide a mid-point but to urge your respondents to avoid using it unless it is the only answer that really reflects their views.

Ranking to show preference

One form of item available to designers of questionnaires is that which requires the respondent to rank a number of terms or concepts in order of importance, eg

Place a number from 1 to 7 in the left hand column opposite each item indicating its importance in your choice of a summer holiday (1 for the most important, 7 for the least important):

☐ plenty of activities
☐ low price
☐ facilities for children
☐ English-speaking country
☐ warm weather
☐ gourmet food
☐ convenient flight times.

The attraction of ranked items is that they appear to cover many points in a single question, saving space and time. However, they suffer from serious disadvantages.

a Analysis of ranked data is limited to a small number of rather complex techniques.

b The importance of each factor is known only in terms of the others; there is no absolute measure. Thus the factor that came out fifth in importance on average might, or might not, be regarded as important by respondents.

c Respondents are slower to decide on their ranking than if they had to say individually how important each factor is; by the time they are ranking the last few items they may be losing patience and not give these items enough thought.

d The ranking might omit important factors that one might not think of at first that would alter the whole set of scores if included.

In short, the apparent convenience of asking about many factors in one short ranking question is often offset by loss of information for the researcher and inconvenience for the respondent.

 Activity 14.1

Now answer these review questions on forms of item. (The solutions are on page 99.)

a Which of the items below would be the more informative?
- How tall are you? Very tall/tall/average height/short/very short
- How tall are you, to the nearest inch?

b True or false? Responses to closed questions are easier to analyse than responses to open questions.

c True or false? Open questions are usually answered more quickly than closed ones.

d What name is given to the type of item that consists of a statement in regard to which respondents indicate their strength of agreement or disagreement by choosing the point with the appropriate wording along a scale?

e True or false? In the great majority of cases it is good practice to provide no mid-point among the responses to choose from so that respondents will not be able to take the easy way out of a difficult question.

f Which type of scaled item is the following?
   Rich   5——4——3——2——1   *Poor*

g Fill in the missing word: *Rich–poor is one of the ...... measured by the scale.*

h True or false? Respondents usually find semantic differential scales easy to understand.

i True or false? Items requiring respondents to rank different elements have the advantage of being easy to analyse.

15 Content of items

Avoiding response set

Response set is the term used for a respondent's tendency to get into a rut by answering all the items in the same way, resulting in a visible alignment of responses in a roughly vertical line, either over to one side or down the middle. The danger is that, after answering several items in the same position along the scale, respondents will expect their view to fall in that position and not give each item due thought.

To avoid this, and also to avoid apparent bias, try to design your items so that a respondent with a strong view in one direction, eg hostile to the object of the attitude, would mark half the items on the left side and half on the right. This would mean that, if respondents are asked how much they agree or disagree with statements, half the statements would be favourable and half unfavourable. (In agree/disagree items the scales should be arranged so that agreement is always consistently indicated at the same end, either left or right.)

The management of your host organisation might object to your prompting respondents with unfavourable statements, but you can explain that, if all statements pointed in the same direction (favourable or unfavourable), this could influence respondents, causing bias in the results. Anyway, you might add, respondents have the option of disagreeing strongly with unfavourable statements.

It is possible to add scores on a series of dimensions, or average them, for an overall figure. However, in doing so you are giving equal weight to each dimension, which may not be appropriate. In any case, there will be a separate analysis of each dimension, so an overall figure runs a serious risk of being either meaningless or misleading.

If you nevertheless intend to add the responses to get an overall score, be sure to be consistent in coding in such a way that the favourable end is always the high score or always the low.

 Activity 15.1

If the previous section is clear you should have no trouble answering the following. (The solutions are on page 99.)

    a True or false? It is good design to place the *Agree* end of the scale either always to the left or always to the right.

    b In designing statements about an object of an attitude, one should make the statements

- always favourable to the object;
- always unfavourable to the object;
- half favourable and half unfavourable;
- all favourable or all unfavourable, depending on the views of the host organisation.

c Why is it desirable to avoid response set?

d True or false? Agreement should consistently correspond to either the high code value or the low code value, particularly when an overall score is going to be calculated.

Components of attitudes

It helps analysis of attitudes to distinguish between various components in the attitude, because these have implications for what you might want to do to change the attitude. One form of analysis is to divide the attitude into:
- beliefs as to facts;
- emotions aroused by the object of the attitude;
- action tendencies regarding the object.

For example, consider attitudes to dogs.

Factual element

'By licking your face dogs can spread a disease leading to blindness.'
Note that a so-called factual element may not be true; indeed, the more interesting ones are not true, as they then show how an attitude may be changed by effective presentation of factual information.

Emotional element

'I am afraid of Rottweilers.'
The essential characteristic of an emotional element is that the object of the attitude arouses a definable emotion in the respondent (in this case, fear). Irrational statements, such as *'Women cannot drive bulldozers'*, are best classified as factual rather than emotional, though they may indicate an underlying emotion worth exploring with other questions. Emotions aroused by a particular object are seldom changed by persuasion or argument. It requires experience of a different emotion in the presence of the object, for example, in the above case, being induced to make friends with an amiable Rottweiler.

Action tendency

'I would cross the street to avoid passing a child walking a dog on a leash.'
An action-tendency statement says what the respondent would do when confronted

with certain objects of the attitude. Action tendencies are sometimes changed by persuading the person to experiment with a different form of behaviour, eg to go walking with a competent child in charge of a dog.

 Activity 15.2

To practise making the distinction between these three types of item, consider the following and classify them as factual, emotional or action-tendency items. (The solutions are on page 99.)

a Flying causes more air pollution per passenger mile than other forms of transport.
b When taking off in a plane I feel tense.
c I am likely to fly when going on my next holiday.

Common types of faulty items

There are several types of defective questions commonly found in questionnaires, even in those presented with elaborate graphics. Many of these can be identified from your own experience and common sense.

 Activity 15.3

See if you can spot the defects in the examples below. For simplicity the form of response is not shown for most items.

a How do you rate the efficiency and friendliness of the reception staff?
b Do you work or are you a housewife? (Respondent is known to be female.)
c Have you been under stress at work lately?
d In the UK, more men than women are in senior management. (Agree/disagree)
e I would choose a holiday in Spain because I like Spanish food. True or false?
f Marital status? Single/married/divorced.
g Would you prefer to buy a computer through a retail outlet rather than by mail order?
h The customs officer was not unreasonable. (Agree/disagree)

Activity 15.3 – solution

Here are the reasons why the itens above were poor.

a This is a double question, one of the most common forms of error. It is sometimes used in an effort to shorten a questionnaire, but the answer to one half of the question (eg efficiency) may well be different from the answer to the other half (friendliness). *Avoid double questions*, which can cause resistance to answering and work against clear responses.

b This is an offensive question to some women, as housework is work. *Avoid potentially offensive questions.*

c The word *lately* is imprecise. Use a specific time span, such as *at any time in the last two weeks. Distances, frequency of occurrence, pay and other such data should be quantified whenever possible.*

d This is such a well-known fact that you can predict the answer. Therefore the question is unnecessary. *Avoid questions where the answer for virtually every respondent would be the same.*

e This is a less obvious form of the double question. The respondent may choose a holiday in Spain despite a dislike for Spanish food. The item could be rephrased to ask how important food is in the respondent's choice of country for a holiday, or to ask for an opinion regarding Spanish food.

f Several other forms of marital status are omitted, eg widowed, separated, unmarried partner etc. When you cannot foresee all possible answers to a question, or when some answers are relatively infrequent or irrelevant, you should include the catch-all option *Other. The range of response options should cover all possible answers.*

g *Keep the language simple.* Not everyone immediately knows the meaning of *retail outlet.* Call it a shop. Another problem with this item: there are other ways to buy a computer, eg from the factory.

h *Avoid negative statements in true/false or agree/disagree items.* This is a particularly confusing item as it is a double negative. It would have been better to say *The customs officer was reasonable.* In general it is better to use such expressions as *I would avoid* ... rather than *I would not be willing to* ...

16 The covering letter

Respondents to a questionnaire need an explanation of why they should cooperate by completing it. This usually calls for a covering letter, though sometimes a questionnaire circulating within an organisation is sufficiently self-explanatory to require only a few introductory lines at the beginning of the questionnaire itself.

The usual contents of a covering letter are as follows:
a Why the survey is being conducted.
b Who is sponsoring it or who has authorised it.
c Who is doing it.
d Why the respondent should fill it in.
e How soon the completed questionnaire is needed.
f What is going to happen to the findings.
g How the respondent's privacy will be respected through anonymity or confidentiality.
h Thanks for cooperation.

Although surveys by students are normally done as part of a coursework requirement, it is usually preferable to justify the questionnaire in its own right, as a matter of interest or general concern, rather than merely as a means of obtaining an academic qualification. The academic connection can be presented as an opportunity to make a useful investigation. If your survey is taking place inside an organisation it should be made clear that it is being conducted with the approval of senior management.

The potential respondent should be given reasons why he or she should complete the questionnaire, either for personal benefit or because it will bring benefits to others. It is better to focus on their needs rather than your own. It is sometimes worth considering offering respondents a copy of the findings as an incentive to reply, but you should be sure that you have the means, funding and approval to do this before offering it.

The covering letter is the place to explain what provision you have made for protecting the privacy of the respondent through confidentiality or anonymity, as discussed in Chapter 12, page 70.

Directions for returning the completed questionnaire should be given at the end of the questionnaire, when they are needed, rather than in the covering letter.

If potential respondents are allowed to opt out and respondents are, in effect, all volunteers, your sample ceases to be random and the percentages you find giving each answer may not be representative of the whole population, as already discussed in Chapter 12. It is important, therefore, to get a reply from everyone in your sample. It may encourage a reply to tell potential respondents that, as a sample, they represent the views of people like themselves.

Practice varies as to whether to state a deadline by which the completed question-naire should be returned. If you give plenty of time, such as two weeks, people tend to put it off and then forget it. If too little, such as two days, they may be offended by your apparent assumption that they have enough spare time to do it immediately. If you set a deadline and people overrun it they may tell themselves that it is too late to send it in anyway. Then when they receive a follow-up a few days after the deadline, they may conclude that it was not a serious deadline after all. Given all these problems with deadlines, you may well decide to ask people to return the questionnaire in the next few days.

Finally, thank them for their cooperation.

Activity 16.1

There are many factors to be taken into account in a good covering letter. This example illustrates many of the potential defects, but unfortunately is all too typical of student covering letters. See how many inadequacies you can spot.

---

21 Torag Lane
Lesser Waffle
Tippleton
ZY17 3PQ

21 November 1992

Dear Manager,

As part of my BABS course I am required to do a project and have chosen to investigate the role of company cars in motivating staff.

Please complete the enclosed questionnaire, giving me your views on this important topic.

The findings will be kept confidential and your name will not be disclosed to anyone except my project supervisor.

I would appreciate it if you could return your reply by 13 December 1992 in the enclosed stamped envelope with any additional information you may wish to offer.

Yours sincerely,

A. Student

Activity 16.1 – solution

This letter fails to do many of the things recommended above.

a It presents itself as primarily a student project, rather than something worthwhile in its own right.

b It does not mention that distribution to managers in the organisation has been authorised by senior management, which it should have been, considering the topic.

c It does not introduce the student adequately. Which year is he or she in, at what institution? BABS is not spelled out as BA Business Studies.

d Does the study fit into a larger research project, eg one being conducted by a lecturer in human resource management? It is always a good idea to link student projects to 'serious' work if possible, both for quality and for interest.

e What will the respondent gain by cooperating? At the very least, contributing to an important activity, at best a summary of the findings.

f Why can the respondent not remain anonymous? If there are good reasons, give them (eg follow-up on interesting comments), or at least give the option of anonymity.

g The deadline is rather abruptly set. It may not be wise to set a deadline, particularly one three weeks ahead.

h The potential respondent is not thanked for helping.

A good covering letter might look something like the following:

Dear Manager,

Here at (Business department of university/college) we need your help.

A research project under Prof. Wilkins is examining the impact of the use of company cars on British industry, funded by the Social Sciences Research Council, and has enlisted student help in assessing the motivating effect of company cars.

I am a fourth-year student on the BA Business Studies course. We have obtained permission from the Human Resource Director of your firm to approach a sample of individual managers like yourself for your views on this topic, estimating that it will take about ten minutes to complete the questionnaire.

Rest assured that once the data have been entered into our database all links between your name and your reply will be removed, and of course your views will not be revealed to your colleagues.

We hope you will want to collaborate in this investigation. If you tick the appropriate box at the end of the questionnaire and provide your name and address, we shall be happy to send you a summary of the results of this questionnaire when they are published (planned for June 1993).

If you are able to give us the benefit of your views by returning the completed questionnaire in the next few days, please accept our thanks.

Sincerely,

(signed legibly, including first name for a friendly tone)

A. Student
BA Business Studies Year 4, Business department of university/college

17 Piloting, distribution and return

Piloting the first version

No matter how much time pressure is on you to get the questionnaire out, you cannot afford to skip piloting it. *Piloting* is the term for trying out a questionnaire on typical respondents. Before sending out hundreds of copies of a questionnaire, a pilot run of 20 or 30 might be advisable, but in the case of student projects piloting usually means giving a presentable copy of the first draft individually to two or three typical respondents to complete while you sit alongside them.

For this purpose you need people who are of ability and background similar to your target population and who are willing to think aloud while filling it in. Your role is to note down any perceived ambiguity or lack of clarity for rewording, and possibly repiloting. Personal friends are often suitable respondents for piloting; be sure to get them to be critical.

Be prepared for some frustration and disappointment at this stage. It is no use arguing with your respondents that they should have understood your instructions or your question. *They* are the ultimate judges of what is clear and what is not. When your facilities permit, it is often a good idea to revise the draft after each piloting respondent has commented, trying out the revised version on the next pilot respondent.

Unfortunately, by sitting alongside the respondents and even discussing the questions with them you have ruined them as respondents for your survey in its final form. Methodological purity requires you to exclude their responses from the final analysis. You should not include them among the respondents to your final version, as your contact with them will probably have altered their views, so they are no longer suitable for a representative sample.

If you make substantial changes to a version of your questionnaire you should pilot it again, or at least pilot the parts changed.

Distribution and return

Distribution within an organisation can sometimes be done through supervisors, and the replies may be collected the same way provided you can ensure confidentiality, for example by providing a blank envelope in which to seal the completed questionnaire.

Respondents should not have to bear postage costs of getting their replies back to you. Indeed, they are unlikely to reply at all if it is going to cost them money as well as time. Using the Royal Mail's Business Reply Service, with reply-paid envelopes, encourages a response. Although some research has shown that envelopes with stamps stuck on get a slightly higher response rate than pre-paid envelopes, adhesive stamps, if used at all, are probably best reserved for the follow-up.

It is very rare to get a 100 per cent response to your first mailing, so plan a follow-up from the beginning by having the covering follow-up letter already written. If you have a way of knowing who has replied, send the follow-up only to those who have not. Otherwise you will need to send it to all the original recipients, asking those who have already replied not to do so again.

Enclose a new copy of the questionnaire unless there is a risk that some respondents may try to pack the ballot box by each filling in more than one questionnaire.

The timing of the follow-up is difficult to predetermine. It is best done when the plotted curve of the cumulative number of responses is beginning to flatten out, as shown in Figure 1. Any subsequent follow-up should be timed in the same way.

Figure 1

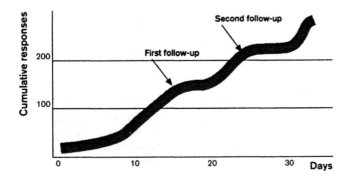

A preview of analysis

Unless you are doing a qualitative analysis of only 20 or 30 responses you will use a computer to compile the results – hence the emphasis on pre-coding to reduce the workload to a minimum.

Upon opening the replies inspect each one for adequate completion. Some respondents may have skipped questions. Your data processing system will provide a code for you to indicate this for processing purposes. Others may have completed it capriciously or maliciously, for example by ticking all the options in the same column at the left, centre or right. Such responses can only be discarded.

Write the case number on each usable response in the space you have previously designated *For office use.*

You can set up the framework for analysis while waiting for the responses to come in. Even with preplanned analysis you will probably want to make additional analyses to explore connections that emerged only after the first pass; allow time for these.

 Activity 17.1

Finally, here is a quiz on the main points of this chapter. (The solutions are on page 99.)

a True or false? With a 60 per cent response rate you can be confident that the replies you have are percentually representative of the whole population being surveyed, making a follow-up unnecessary.

b How do you know when to send out the follow-up?

c True or false? Research has shown that the response rate for Business Reply Service envelopes is as high as it is for stamped envelopes.

d True or false? A completed questionnaire in which the respondent has skipped one or more items should be discarded.

e What is the first thing you do upon opening the envelope containing a completed questionnaire?

f What is the correct term for the sequential number you write on each adequately completed questionnaire to identify it?

18 Conclusion

You now have the basic knowledge needed to make a good first attempt at questionnaire design and distribution. However, you will recognise that these are complex skills that need practice to be perfected. Experience will show you how your best-laid plans, even when carefully guided by these notes, can go wrong when your ultimate critics, your respondents, deliver their verdict.

Further reading is offered in Chapter 19. You will also need to brief yourself on choosing an appropriate method of data collection (which may well turn out *not* to be a questionnaire, see Chapter 7), how to calculate sample size (see Chapter 9), and how to analyse the responses. If you are not already familiar with the vast statistical resources modern computing puts at your disposal, consult a knowledgeable person – *before* you finalise the design of your questionnaire – on how to analyse each item. This should spare you the all-too-common lament from such people: *If only you had come to me earlier!*

Now all that remains is to wish you good luck with your questionnaire!

---

19 Bibliography

Bell, J. (1987) *Doing your research project,* Milton Keynes, Open University Press.

Breakwell, G. M. (1990) *Interviewing,* Leicester, British Psychological Society.

Converse, J. and Presser, S. (1986) *Survey questions, handcrafting the standardized questionnaire,* Beverly Hills, CA, Sage.

Crouch, S. (1984) *Marketing research for managers,* London, Heinemann.

Likert, R. (1961) *New patterns of management,* New York, McGraw-Hill.

Market Research Society (1984) *Standardised questions, a review for market research executives,* London, Market Research Society.

Oppenheim, A. N. (1992) *Questionnaire design, interviewing and attitude measurement,* London, Pinter.

Reeves, T. K. and Harper, D. (1981) *Surveys at work, student project manual,* Maidenhead, McGraw-Hill.

Sekaran, U. (1992) *Research methods for business,* (2nd ed.), New York, Wiley.

Solutions to activities

Activity 12.1

a Qualitative.
b Qualitative.
c True.
d Qualitative.
e qualITATIVE, quantITATIVE.

Activity 13.3

a Case number.
b Item.
c False. Having to give their name could put them off.
d False. Sensitive questions are best surrounded by more straightforward ones.
e True. The respondent needs to concentrate on the subject matter, not on adapting to constantly changing forms of response.
f False. It usually complicates analysis.
g False. They should be placed on the right hand side of the page.
h False. The item numbers go on the left.
i Open questions to capture overlooked points, or perhaps name and address for follow-up if respondent is willing.

Activity 14.1

a How tall are you, to the nearest inch?
b True.
c False.
d Likert-type item.
e False. There is no general clear advantage in either having a mid-point or not having one.
f Semantic differential.

g Dimensions.
h True.
i False. Ranked data are difficult to analyse.

Activity 15.1

a True. It avoids confusing the respondent.
b Half favourable and half unfavourable, to avoid response set.
c To encourage the respondent to think carefully about each item.
d False. The coding should accompany the favourability of the responses, not agreement or disagreement.

Activity 15.2

a Factual.
b Emotional.
c Action-tendency.

Activity 17.1

a False.
b When the plotted response curve begins to flatten out.
c False.
d False.
e Check to see whether it has been completed adequately (ie conscientiously, though possibly not completely).
f Case number.

Part D: Research interviews

Introduction

This part aims to develop your skills in understanding and managing research interviews. It has been designed to encourage you to consider systematically key aspects of the interview as a research tool – its potential, its execution and its aftermath.

Objectives

On completion of the exercises in this part, you should be able to:
- evaluate the status of interviews as a method of research and investigation;
- apply and assess some of the key skills and techniques involved in interviewing and interview management;
- understand the strategic use of interviews in the context of differing types and styles of research and enquiry.

In our context, interviews are understood to be one of a range of survey and investigation techniques which can play a vital part in the systematic practice of 'finding out' or researching information and exploring many aspects of the social world. While this part develops a specific focus on the research interview, it is worth beginning by noting that we have all probably experienced interviews – maybe more often as the interviewee than as the interviewer, conventionally answering, rather than asking the questions.

Questions and answers are the most basic currency of interviews as they are in much of everyday conversation and communication. However, we do not tend to think of the familiar interactions and conversations with friends or family as regular, extended interviews. Instead, interviews are generally understood as particular, formalised events which carry with them different and distinctive meanings in the ways their basic components – the questions and answers – are organised and interact. This formality may be related to a number of factors and conditions. These include:

- **setting**. Where does the interview take place (physical and cultural surroundings)?

- **context**. What is at stake in the interview (the conditions under which those involved participate)?

- **topic**.What is the subject of the questions and who asks them?

- **relations**.Do the participants have equal stakes in the conduct of the interview, who sets the agenda and on what basis?

- **performance**. How are these factors negotiated 'on the day', during the interview, by all parties involved?

Interviews have become an accepted if not normal part of bureaucratic and organisational life. Perhaps one of their widest applications is in the selection of people for jobs or access to other arena, eg in education. They are a fundamental device within broadcast and other media, in news or current affairs programmes for example. Typically they are accompanied by the clipboard: in the street, supermarket, at the door, or on the phone. They have also become a major part of market research, public opinion polling and other forms of social and commercial enquiry. It is assumed that you are involved in a relatively small-scale research project connected with a particular stage of your course and studies. You will get more out of the activites if you are able to work with a small group or another person. You will find it useful to refer to other chapters in this book.

Preliminary activity

Consider three interview situations that you have recently encountered or been involved in. List them in the first row of a 7-row table in a notebook.

In the next six rows of the table, note down their most significant and common features, eg where they took place, why you attended, how you felt before and after, what types of questions you had to deal with.

Compare your notes with other students if you can. There may be some interesting differences and similarities.

20 The research interview – some key issues

Interviews as research methods

Interviews are a research technique which can be used in investigating a wide variety of research problems and projects. In certain circumstances they may be the sole method employed in generating data and information or they may be used as part of a battery of methods in the investigation of selected aspects of a common problem.

Interviewing is rarely a spontaneous activity for the researcher. Prior to any research involving interviewing careful planning and thoughtful preparation are essential. Productive interviews are usually the result of careful, pre-interview research. One of the most important initial questions facing you, the researcher, concerns when to interview – in relation to what kinds of research problem? This question is linked with some related issues – why should interviews be used as a research method, how will they distinctively contribute to the project or your knowledge of the problem under investigation?

Closely related here is the question of whom to interview. This in turn poses a further series of questions relating to the style of interview to be employed – what type of interview is best adopted and why?

 Activity 20.1

In considering the use of interviews in your research, you will need to address the following questions. Make some initial notes now and return to them as you need to.
  a Why should I use interviews?
  b How will interviews contribute to my project?
  c Whom should I interview?
  d What type of interview will I use?
  e How many interviews do I need?
  f How will I record the interviews?
  g How will I assess the results of the interviews?

Variations in the research interview

It is useful to think of research interviews as ranging along a scale or continuum which encompasses a number of possibilities: from the *formal survey interview* to interviews which may be much *less formal* in style. A central issue here will concern your research aims and the problem you have decided to tackle. If your aim is primarily to measure what you are studying and to express your findings in statistical, quantitative form – as numbers – you are likely to want to adopt the formal, survey interview. If, on the other hand, your concern is qualitative in its aim to explore or gain insight into the social meanings or cultural significance of a particular issue or topic, you may find that a less formal type of interview offers the most appropriate method.

Types of interview may differ on a number of counts. These would include:

a scale (large or small number, or sample, of interviewees);
b scope (general or focused content or topic areas);
c time (long or short interviews, retrospective or contemporary in focus, etc).

These different types all involve transactions – forms of exchange or negotiation – between a researcher seeking forms of information on the one hand and, on the other, a subject – or group of subjects, the people interviewed – who may supply relevant information in response to the researcher's questions. It is useful to think of questions as assuming two main forms – *open* or *closed*.

Closed questions

These are designed and tend to be asked in order to get at specific facts, figures or information, where the interviewer tightly controls the terms of the interviewee's answer – 'closing' down the possibilities for the interviewee to volunteer all sorts of information. The questions direct the interviewee towards a particular type of response, eg:

* How many years have you lived in Leicester?
* Do you own a word-processor?
* How many times have you visited the cinema in the last six months?
* When did you leave school?
* What is your age?

 Activity 20.2

Note down some closed questions that you may need to ask in relation to your own research. Remember, the aim of these questions is to pin-point certain factual or measurable forms of information.

Open questions

In contrast to the closed question, open questions are typically less directed towards specific factual or yes/no predetermined types of response. Open questions seek to give the interviewee much more initiative in terms of how they might respond. Typically they operate to elicit responses which are more discursive, concerning the interviewee's personal evaluation or attitudes towards a given issue or event. The open form of question gives the interviewee more space in which to work in responding; more room to relate their views, ideas, values, feelings, attitudes, motives and so on.

For example:

- How did you feel when you first discovered that you were pregnant?
- What would you like to be doing at work in five years' time?
- Why did you decide to change career at that stage?
- What do you feel about current attempts to improve the local environment?
- What do you think is the likely outcome of the new working arrangements?
- What are your earliest memories of life in the village?

 Activity 20.3

Note down some ideas for open questions that you may need to ask in relation to your own research. Remember that these will be designed to gain personal forms of insight or attitudes relevant to the topic.

Some types of interview will tend to use the closed format more or less exclusively, especially if it is part of a quantitative survey. Others may employ a mix of the two types and some may use mainly open-ended or non-directive forms of question in a more conversational, naturalistic and qualitative approach.

 Activity 20.4

At this stage, you may find it useful to note down some of the key questions that you are setting out to answer in your own research projects. On the basis of the discussion so far, what type of interview will best achieve your aims – the formal or the less formal?

Types of research interview

Given the range of options open to the research interviewer you might find it useful to think of a continuum which embraces the extremes *formal survey interviews* and *less formal interviews*.

Formal survey interviews

These are transactions in which a sequence of carefully preplanned and piloted set questions are asked and the answers recorded on a standardised schedule. The questions will tend to be closed and directed. Here is an example, taken from a recent interview schedule designed to research viewers' attitudes towards particular programmes, in this case, the BBC 2 programme *Have I Got News For You*.

1 Have you seen any of the recent series of this current-affairs quiz show?
    1 Yes (Please answer questions 3 to 6.)
    2 No (Please answer question 2 only.)

2 Why have you not watched any of this series?
    1 Didn't know it was on
    2 Programme didn't appeal to me
    3 I preferred to watch another channel/video
    4 Not a convenient time for me to watch TV
    5 Someone else chose not to watch

3 Why did you watch *Have I Got News For You*?
(You may circle more than one number.)
    1 Enjoyed previous series
    2 Attracted by TV trailer
    3 Attracted by something I read
    4 They had guest(s) on that I liked
    5 The TV happened to be on
    6 Nothing on other channels
    7 Someone else chose to watch
    8 Other reasons

4 How much do you agree or disagree with each of these statements about the programme?
(Please use the following scale where 5 = Agree strongly, 4 = Agree, 3 = Neither agree nor disagree, 2 = Disagree, 1 = Disagree strongly.)

Boring	5	4	3	2	1
One of my favourite programmes	5	4	3	2	1
Appeals to my sense of humour	5	4	3	2	1
I sometimes laugh out loud when watching	5	4	3	2	1
Some of the things they say are too cruel	5	4	3	2	1
I like it when they really have a go at people	5	4	3	2	1
The host and captains work well together	5	4	3	2	1
Too many comments about the same people	5	4	3	2	1
Good choice of guests	5	4	3	2	1
The guests didn't say enough	5	4	3	2	1
I tried to watch it every week	5	4	3	2	1
I would like to see another series	5	4	3	2	1

5 Using the same scale, how much do you agree with these statements about the host, Angus Deayton, and the captains, Paul Merton and Ian Hislop?
    a Angus Deayton
    b Ian Hislop
    c Paul Merton

Likeable	5	4	3	2	1
Too smug	5	4	3	2	1
Amusing	5	4	3	2	1
Too sarcastic	5	4	3	2	1
Quick witted	5	4	3	2	1
Irritating	5	4	3	2	1

As you can see by the way that it aims to 'pigeon hole' responses, this kind of interview is similar to a verbally delivered questionnaire, and you will find it discussed in more detail in Chapter 21. Also, have a look at Part C: Questionnaire design.

Less formal interviews

In these types of interview situation the interviewer has the freedom to modify the sequence of questions, change the wording and, to a limited extent, probe or extend aspects of the interviewee's responses. The interviewer is still formally in control of the questions, which may tend to include more open-ended forms. As a result, in places the interview may tend to be less directed and more conversational. However, although interviewer and interviewee have more freedom in which to work, the researcher's schedule of questions will still control the interview. Some researchers have dispensed with even this control and have opted for an interview style which is defined by an absence of explicit, formal structure and direction on the part of the interviewer, who may simply work to a number of key themes which are raised in a conversational, relaxed fashion. Questions will tend to be open ended, prompts for maintaining or stimulating response, rather than seeking predictable, closed facts or figures. Interviewee and interviewer have much more space to 'ad lib' or work around topics which may shift according to the interviewee's direction, not just that of the interviewer. In certain circumstances, this may mean that the interviewer's role or power to set and move the agenda will almost disappear as he or she becomes subordinate to the responses and discussion initiated by the interviewee.

The use of these types of interview is discussed in more detail in Chapter 22.

 Activity 20.5

Below are a number of research problems. What types of interviews might you conduct in exploring them? Bear in mind the styles of formal or less formal interviews outlined earlier. Also, note the types and numbers of people you would aim to interview. What might the chosen interview method provide that other methods would not be able to get at?

  a   A study of British attitudes towards Europe and European integration.

  b   An analysis of alcohol consumption among young men and women aged 16–24 years.

c A study of weekend leisure patterns among college/university students.
d An investigation into current patterns of musical consumption by selected youth groups.
e A study of memories of primary school experiences.
f An investigation into student attitudes towards different styles of lecturing and assessment.

 Activity 20.6

For this exercise you will need to work with a fellow student and take turns in playing the roles of interviewer and interviewee. Both of you should nominate topics on which you would like to be interviewed (these might refer to any particular interests or recent experiences). Each of you take some time to design between six and ten questions on the topic chosen by your partner. With reference to the types of interview outlined above, take turns in carrying out the interviews. Note down any issues which you feel are significant in playing the roles of interviewer and interviewee. Also consider any problems which occur and any general conclusions you might reach about the value of using interviews as research techniques. You might find it useful to repeat this exercise at a later stage, using a topic relevant to your intended research project.

 Activity 20.7

One form of interview that we are familiar with is the interview on radio or television. This is a device widely used by broadcasters to relay diverse forms of information and opinion to audiences. In developing an awareness of research interviewing you will find that it is worth spending time considering some of the types of interview that we encounter on a daily basis in the context of radio or television programmes. These provide a useful source of material for considering some of the techniques and problems involved in interviews when used as a research method. For this activity you will need to record a selected number of interviews from radio or television news or current affairs programmes – for example *Today* on BBC Radio Four or *Newsnight* on BBC 2. Analyse the ways in which the questions and answers are 'balanced' and how the interviewer manages the proceedings. Note down any issues that you think are important about the conduct or format of the broadcast interview. How do broadcast interviews differ from research interviews?

The research interview – strengths and weaknesses

A consistent theme in the literature of research interviewing concerns the basic point that if you want to know something about people's activities, the best way of finding out is to ask them. In the research interview, it is argued, the researcher has direct access to unique forms of expertise and experience which are often not accessible by means of other research methods. Some proponents of this view emphasise the ways in which the processes and theories underpinning research interviewing treat individuals and groups as able to supply insightful and valuable accounts of their own actions.

From this point of view, interviews are regarded as essential for any kind of research which attempts to go beyond simple measurement of the occurrence or existence of social phenomena. Interviews are able to provide the researcher with important quantitative data at this basic level of analysis – for example in researching the percentage of women university students who drive a car. However, they are also the means whereby the researcher can go further, in gaining deeper, qualitative insight into the meanings that people attribute to, or derive from, their participation in events and situations, for example in a project which explores differing shades of opinion in response to new environmental initiatives in the city centre.

In this respect research interviewers may tend to emphasise the importance of the interview process as a means of genuinely understanding and coming to terms with the social dimension in any research. The subjects of interviews – selected people or groups – are regarded as invaluable sources of information, and the interview offers the possibility of direct communication with them.

 Activity 20.8

From what you have read so far, list the strengths of the research interview in general. Make your own notes and then read the summary.

Summary of strengths

The strengths of the interview are conventionally identified by comparison with other research methods, for example the questionnaire. These include:

a **Freedom**. Both parties – researcher and researched – are allowed to explore the meaning of questions and negotiate the topic under study.

b **Directness of contact and feedback**. Misunderstandings on the part of the interviewee can be checked immediately.

c **Speed of response**. Interviews can be conducted on a day-to-day frequency, to capture changes in opinion, etc.

d **Extensive range of data and topics**. Many issues can be encompassed in the same interview.

e **Interview data may usefully confirm or disconfirm findings from other sources**. Subject to validity and reliability checks, interview data may be generalised from the sample studied to more general populations – from car drivers in Leicestershire to those in the United Kingdom as a whole for example.

Many writers and researchers have also noted a range of *weaknesses* that may disadvantage the researcher using interview methods. List the weaknesses of research which has employed interview methods. Make your own notes and then read the summary.

Summary of weaknesses

The weaknesses typically identified in projects which have used interviews include:

a **Bias and distortion during the interview**. Precisely because the contact between interviewer and interviewee is of a face-to-face, direct nature, there are many ways in which bias may occur. For example, in the context of issues or questions which cover sensitive or private matters, the interviewee may evade or avoid questions. Interviewee responses may not always be as reliable or trustworthy as is often assumed. This may be for a variety of reasons, including poor memory recall, exaggeration, or a respondent who tries too hard to give the interviewer what he or she thinks they want. For these and other reasons the data collected by means of interview may be invalidated or questionable.

b **Cost and inconsistency**. Large-scale, formal survey interviews depend on large teams of trained interviewers. This increases the cost of interviewing relative to other methods and may also introduce greater possibilities for unwanted variations to appear in the interview process as a whole.

c **Margins of error and misunderstanding.** Errors and distortions may also arise at the point when interview data is interpreted or made sense of after interviews have taken place. There are issues concerning how far responses can be taken as representative; in other words, mirroring those of people in general, beyond those who were actually involved in the interview process. In dealing with verbal responses, interviews generate a complex mass of verbal information, which in its recorded or transcribed form is always open to a number of misunderstandings or contradictory readings on the part of the researcher.

Conclusion

This section has introduced you to some key questions concerning the use of research interviews. We now turn to develop some of these by addressing the procedures involved in designing and carrying out formal survey interviews.

21 Formal survey interviews

This is a style of research interviewing which is usually designed to generate a large, reliable amount of representative and quantitative data. It is, as suggested earlier, rather like a verbal or 'talking' questionnaire. It is also the type of interview method which would tend to be associated with gathering facts, measuring or 'mapping' patterns of behaviour or attitude rather than analysing them in great detail. You will find it useful to refer to Part C: Questionnaire design, in conjunction with this chapter. At the heart of the survey interview project is the schedule of questions to be administered.

Constructing the schedule

The schedule is the basic script for all of the interviews involved in the survey. Combinations of three kinds of question type are usually employed:
  a the fixed alternative question;
  b the scaled question;
  c the open-ended question.

If you use the *fixed alternative* question you require the respondent to choose from two or more predetermined alternatives. The most frequently employed form is the yes/no, true/false, agree/disagree type. In some circumstances you may find it useful to extend these positive/ negative options by adding a third alternative such as 'don't know' or 'undecided'.

Example
Do you think that compact discs have improved the quality of music?
  ☐ Yes
  ☐ No
  ☐ Don't know.

In addition to these types of question there are other ways of presenting interviewees with fixed alternatives. One method, often referred to as the checklist, requires the respondent to select one from a range of alternatives.

Example
I derive most satisfaction at university/college from:
  ☐ lectures
  ☐ seminars
  ☐ the social life
  ☐ student societies
  ☐ studying on my own.

There are a number of advantages and disadvantages in using fixed alternative questions. They have, for example, the advantage of producing greater uniformity and hence greater reliability. This is achieved partly because respondents are forced to answer in a way which fits only the categories of response available. These kinds of questions are also easily coded, that is, given numerical values for statistical computerised analysis. Principal disadvantages would include the fact that they are often superficial. Respondents will often get irritated when none of the alternatives given appear to match their views. This may result in the possibility of responses which are inappropriate, inaccurate or misleading.

The scaled format is a development of the fixed alternative form which allows the interviewee to respond to a question or a statement by registering degrees of agreement or disagreement, or according to other chosen dimensions. The response is invited on a set scale or continuum.

Example
Do you think that smoking should be banned in all public places?
Strongly agree – Agree – Undecided – Disagree – Strongly disagree

How would you rate the services provided by your university library?
Excellent – Good – Fair – Poor – Very poor

The statement form may also be used to elicit responses on a given scale.

Example
How much do you agree or disagree with the following statement?
Advertisements on television interfere with my enjoyment of the programmes.
Strongly agree – Agree – Undecided – Disagree – Strongly disagree.

How much do you agree or disagree with the following statement?
Babies and children should be allowed into British public houses much more than at present.
Strongly agree – Agree – Undecided – Disagree – Strongly disagree.

In some cases it may be appropriate to ask respondents to *rank order* a set of given alternatives. This will require the interviewer to acquaint the interviewee adequately with the possible options.

Example
What are your most important sources of relaxation?
(1 = most important, 5 = least important)
- ☐ Socialising with friends outside of my house.
- ☐ Spending time with my family at home.
- ☐ Participating in a sport.
- ☐ Gardening.
- ☐ Listening to music.

111

Summary

Survey interviews which make use of scaled or ranked responses do add to the options open to the interviewee. Perhaps their prime strength lies in the fact that they do this with a degree of speed and efficiency. They can also be easily quantified or coded for statistical analysis. Against this, you should bear in mind that responses to the scale or rank order are still forced into alternatives which are fixed by you, the researcher, and not the interviewee. These kinds of questions may produce important insights, but their validity crucially depends upon the interviewee accurately understanding the terms of reference that the schedule and interviewer is working within. From this point of view, the distinctions between 'strongly disagreeing' and 'agreeing' or being 'undecided' may be extensive or minimal and may be defined by different respondents along a range of different variables.

Open-ended questions may be employed in formal survey interviews, although it is in the nature of the survey that they will tend to be used with economy and rarely dominate the schedule. As suggested earlier, open forms of question offer a broad frame of reference for interviewees' responses, their views, opinions, feelings, etc. They give the interviewee more space to take the initiative in responding to a given question.

Example
Complete the following:
What kinds of influence do you think that television advertisements have had on you over the years?

Complete the following:
What have been the most stressful experiences for you since you came to university?

Open-ended questions have several *advantages*:
- They allow your interviewee to give their account, without this being forced into categories or options. This may give rise to a greater sense of engagement or rapport between interviewer and interviewee and may lead to more genuine or authentic – and hence valuable – forms of response.
- The questions may also allow the interviewer to probe certain issues or develop a more flexible approach to the interview.

Open-ended questions, however, also introduce *risks* into the procedure:
- People may say all sorts of things, giving unanticipated or unexpected responses. In some cases these may trigger new forms of insight or connection for the research project as a whole, but they may be difficult to record adequately and difficult to code or attach numerical value to. For a useful discussion of this aspect consult Chapter 13, pages 76–81.

- In general, open-ended questions may tend to interrupt or contradict the general aims of the survey interview for specific, manageable and large-scale responses.

Open-ended questions may, however, play an important role in 'punctuating' the interview. They may, in the context of the survey, be employed as a means of establishing or initiating a topic or theme which is then narrowed down through the use of more specific, closed or fixed alternative strategies. This process of limiting and focusing questions has been referred to as the *funnel approach*, in that the interviewer moves from open-ended to closed questions, for example:

'How did you approach choosing a course in Higher Education?'

'Which course and year are you currently enrolled on?'

Stages in the survey process

Having examined the main components which are available to the researcher using formal survey interviews, it is now useful to work through the steps and stages in the survey process as a whole. These are:
- specification
- design
- interviewing
- analysis.

Specification

The initial stage of any interview study will involve you in the clear specification of the purpose and scope of the investigation. This should involve pinning down and clarifying the principal conceptual issues at stake in the study, and defining and making explicit the hypothesis or problem you wish to research. You will need to consider and refine the specific angle you wish to focus on and should be able to list the broad aims of the project. You will find that much of this will be accomplished by reference to other information sources. For example, you may find it useful to examine any similar research or other available data sources which may have relevance for your own work. This will require you to consult available literature and in turn will assist in the process of specifying, breaking down and sequencing your objectives. This is a fundamental part of the overall process and its implications for later stages should not be underestimated. Have another look at the questions posed at the start of Chapter 20 and in Activity 20.1.

If you are involved in a group project, this stage may require some division of labour, but it is essential that all group members share the same precise definition of the aims of the study (see the title *Successful group work* in this series). At this stage, you will certainly need to organise a timetable and evaluate the resources available for your study. Make sure you produce a working plan for the project which is manageable in practical terms.

Design

The second stage involves the design of the interview schedule itself. This entails translating the specified research aims and objectives into the questions which will make up the final schedule. You will need to consider in detail the variables that you want to explore. These are the factors that you want to measure and they will directly relate to the questions you design. At this stage you will need to bear in mind the types and possible combinations of questions available – fixed alternative, scaled or open ended – together with the types of responses that they will elicit. You will need to think carefully through questions aimed to gather factual information and those dealing with opinions. Many interview schedules begin with a section which itemises information about the respondent – their age, gender, occupation, etc. To complete this stage you will need to finalise several related tasks and issues. This will include establishing the particular size of the sample your survey will be based upon (how many interviews will be conducted?). You will also have to consider the type of people you want to interview, the nature of the sample, how to select them and how best to contact them. Consideration will also need to be devoted to the method of recording responses – on paper or tape are the two main forms – although many surveys operate by recording responses on copies of the schedule. If you are going to use a computer to analyse or record data about people you should note the terms of the Data Protection Act (1984) (see Chapter 12, page 71), which set certain constraints on this activity.

These aspects of organising your research will accompany the final writing of questions: designing, sequencing and preparing the completed schedule. An important part of this process should involve *piloting* or testing out the schedule and making any final adjustments or necessary refinements. Piloting is a vital step in the process of perfecting and trying out your schedule and you neglect it at your peril.

Interviewing

The third stage involves the actual interviewing process itself. In the survey interviews you carry out you should aim at consistency throughout. At the point of contact with your interviewees it is usual to brief the respondent as to the purpose of the interview and to try to make them feel at ease. You will need to introduce yourself and clarify how responses are to be recorded. Many people, quite rightly, are sensitive to this issue and you should generally be able to give reassurance concerning the confidentiality of their part in the proceedings.

One of the main challenges facing the survey interviewer is to remain consistent and not to deviate from the schedule unless this allows for a more open-ended, flexible approach. In some cases you will experience difficulties, either in terms of unforeseen events occuring in the interview situation or more generally with regard to topic management or keeping the respondent 'on the track' of the schedule. Practice in this respect may not make perfect but it will improve your technique considerably.

Analysis

Once data from the total number of interviews in the survey has been collected, the final stage – in a sense the real point of the research – begins. This entails the analysis and interpretation of your data in the light of the initial research specification. One part of this process will involve the statistical analysis and presentation of your results. For example, in the context of fixed alternative questions you should be able to calculate percentages of response, say for yes/no/don't know options which have resulted from your total survey population. For scaled questions you should also be able to provide a similar statistical 'map' of the relative strengths of response registered.

For example:
'Do you think that compact discs have improved the quality of music?'

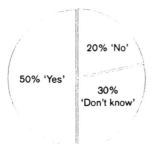

In the context of open-ended questions you should be looking for any recurrent patterns in the data recorded. In all these cases your main problems at this stage will concern interpreting the significance of these patterns in the light of the original research problems and ideas you commenced with. What do these patterns imply? Do they confirm or shed light on your original problem? If you are working within a group on the project you may need to spend some considerable time discussing and evaluating your research process and results as a group. This final stage will also encompass the 'write up' – the writing and presentation of your research results. You may need to check on any specific requirements, word length, etc, which will govern the format of your final presentation.

To assist you with data analysis and the presentation of results, you may find it useful to consult and use a range of computer software packages. Details of these can usually be obtained from the computer services of most universities and colleges.

 Activity 21.1

Design an interview schedule and work through the first two stages outlined above for one or more of the following research topics based where your university/college is sited. You may need to vary, adapt or specify certain aspects.

a Student attitudes towards the leisure facilities and amenities in your town/city.

b Public attitudes towards rail and road transport in your town/city.

c Patterns and preferences for alcoholic drinks and their consumption among young men and women in any one selected occupational group.

d Awareness of safe-sex campaigns among young men and women aged 16–20 years.

e Other examples are provided in Activity 20.5.

22 Less formal interviews

The previous section suggested that the formal survey interview is concerned predominantly with gathering large amounts of data according to a relatively rigid schedule of set questions. Its underlying rationale tends to be one of quantitative measurement in relation to the focus of study. In contrast, less formal types of interview are employed by researchers who will usually spend more time interviewing a smaller number of people in a less directed, less mechanical style, and whose concerns differ in a number of ways.

Researchers opting for less formal interviews are likely to be concerned to produce a qualitative understanding of the topic under study. This means that they will use interviews to gain insight into the meanings, interpretations, values and experiences of the interviewee and his or her 'world'. Implicit in this approach are a number of important assumptions and consequences which, it is worth noting, may proceed from, or indeed accompany, formal survey interviews.

The aims of the less formal interview

Researchers working with less formal interviews adopt a different perspective on the nature of the social world which, they argue, differs from the natural world in that it is composed essentially of meanings, values and interpretations. According to this view people differ from natural objects in their ability to interpret their own actions and those of others, to act on their understandings and to endow their lives and actions with meanings. These are not understood as fixed, 'measurable' entities, but are regarded as actively created and negotiated through social interaction. The task of the interviewer is to create and to adapt to the conditions under which the interviewee will disclose or 'open up' their particular version or unique 'inside story' relevant to the issue under consideration.

As a result, those working within this approach will assume that there are always multiple, widely divergent perspectives held by people concerning the problem or issue under study. Their aims and interview techniques will be concerned to reduce the formality, control and distance often involved in the survey style of interview and to replace this with a more flexible, conversational format. This will entail more emphasis on open-ended, non-directed questions rather than requiring the interviewee to provide specific bits of information in response to fixed alternative questions. The interviewer will not have a schedule of prepared questions, rather a sequence of themes or points to be covered and followed in discussion. The role of the interviewer may tend to be more passive, involving a process of active listening and prompting, rather than administering a list of questions for answers. This kind of interviewing will often accompany forms of observation, in some cases participant observation, where the interviewer participates in the activities or social settings under study. As a result these interviews will tend to be carried out in 'natural' settings and contexts, on 'territory' familiar to the interviewee rather than to the interviewer. In general terms, researchers in this approach will also pay more attention to the process of each interview – including their own part in it – and how this might have implications for the insights and data gathered as a result. This is termed 'reflexivity'. They will act less as 'interrogators' and more as 'guides' in the interview and in the process of mutually 'finding out' about the topics being researched.

 Activity 22.1

In the light of this discussion you may find it useful to note some of the main *differences* between the less formal type of interview compared with the formal survey type. Make your own notes and then read the summary.

The less formal interview contrasts with the survey form in the following ways:

a The interviewer is aiming to 'get inside' the subjective meanings and 'world' of the interviewee. This is a more time-consuming method, capable of revealing greater depth of response.

b The interview will tend to be less formal, more open, flexible and conversational, and it will take place in naturalistic settings.

c The roles of the interviewer and interviewee are defined differently, the interviewer will negotiate and adapt much more with the interviewee in the process of exploring the topics under discussion. In some cases the interviewee will 'set the agenda' much more than the interviewer.

d Rather than working to a set schedule of questions, the interviewer will tend to use a flexible sequence of non-directed questions to trigger or 'steer' the interviewee into talking about broad areas or themes. The interview process will therefore be subject to constant modification.

e The information recorded during the interview will differ considerably. It will be less structured, less predictable and less amenable to statistical analysis and coding. It may be difficult to compare material from different interviews and to use interviews as a basis for generalisation.

 Activity 22.2

In the light of the points above, you may find it useful at this stage to list and recap on some of the *strengths* and *weaknesses* of the less formal versus the formal survey interview styles of research. Use your own research projects and topics as a basis for this exercise. Make your own notes and then read through the summary.

Summary

The principal strengths or advantages of the less formal approach largely concern the ways in which greater depth and insight can be achieved than might be effected within the constraints of the formal survey approach. By employing less formal interview styles the researcher can gain considerable insight into the meanings, motives, values or feelings of the people who consent to participate in interviews. They can 'dig deeper' and the results of this type of research are usually rich in descriptive terms. Where the survey interview may point to the existence of a particular attitude or value, the less formal interview allows you, the researcher, to get to the heart of it.

What is a strength for some, however, may be regarded by others as a weakness. For those researchers working within the formal survey tradition, informal interviews are of questionable value. In particular, there are no explicit or easy mechanisms whereby responses may be compared, measured or generalised about. In pursuit of the 'inside stories', the less formal interview allows for much greater subjective bias – your own values or those of the interviewees – on the part of both participants. In addition, because of the relatively intensive, lengthy duration of the interviews, a smaller number are usually accomplished by comparison with the survey. This provides less of a basis from which to make statistical generalisation. For proponents of the survey approach, the less formal interview may tell us a lot about the particular individual or case, but reveal little about general patterns or trends. Against this, the point of the less formal approach is to obtain a more complete and complex picture of the subject.

It is important to bear in mind two points here. First, the two methods of interviewing have clearly evolved to deal with different types of question and levels of analysis. Both have strengths when applied in the investigation of appropriate problems or research questions. The fundamental issue of quantitative versus qualitative research is a key one which you will have to resolve here. This places emphasis on the researcher developing a clear and explicit rationale for using one or the other method. Second, the two styles of interview may be combined in investigation. Less formal techniques may play an important role in developing a formal survey, and they may provide an important means of furthering investigation of areas too complex for the limitations of the formal survey.

Stages in the less formal interview

There is no one, correct way to conduct a less formal interview. The process will generally require considerably more skill, patience and insight on the part of the interviewer than in the survey situation. The steps in the research procedure are worth comparing with those outlined for the survey (Chapter 21, pages 110–116) and can be summarised as follows: specification; contact; interviewing; analysis.

Specification

This initial, preparatory stage is broadly similar to that outlined for the survey procedure. It should involve the precise definition of the aims of the study, of research on any other sources of relevant information and a general clarification of objectives. You will need to think through the case for utilising less formal interview procedures and should be able to support this choice of method in terms of the subject matter or topic chosen for investigation. What is to be gained by the use of less formal interviews should be clearly established. You will need to finalise your themes and questions for the interviews, as far as possible, at this stage. This should involve some piloting of the proposed sequence.

Contact

You will need to select and contact your potential interviewees. This may involve approaching all, or a selected number, of people in a particular group or location – for example, in the case of a study of a particular work culture. It may, however, mean that you need to get access to a number of families, older people, working women, representatives of a more general type. In these cases you will need to establish a point of contact with your potential interviewees. This may be done by utilising existing networks (for example, tracking magazine readers via a newsagent's list) or by you attending a particular event or meeting (for example of a club or society) in order to develop contacts. As part of this process you will need to be able to outline briefly your research and the subjects you want to talk about in the interview. In general, the interviewer will make himself/herself available to suit the convenience of the interviewee, and it is the interviewee who should also nominate the meeting place. Their own home is generally regarded as one of the best locations, unless there are significant gains to be made 'on site' – at work, in the club, in the school, etc.

Interviewing

There is considerable debate about the most effective ways of recording less formal or informal interviews. The attempt to create varying shades of informality is often undermined or contradicted by the practice of recording what is said. For further advice on recording interviews, see Chapter 23. It is useful to start the interview by making a formal record of the name of the interviewee and any other discreet data relevant to the project. The interviewee should be reassured about the confidentiality of their responses and the nature of the research being undertaken. In very informal interviews both of these steps may be modified considerably. In some circumstances it is also useful to commence by ascertaining how much time is available, so that you can pace the interview accordingly. About one hour is usually regarded as the minimum desirable time for a productive interview. The main questions and themes and a broad sequence will have been prepared and considered in advance, but follow-up questions and discussion cannot be anticipated. You may find that the technique of 'looping' (developing a prompt question from the response just given) is a useful technique for keeping the interviewee 'flowing'. Many researchers have stressed the value of the *follow-up* question in these circumstances.

Analysis

Having completed as many interviews as possible and depending upon which method has been employed for recording the interviews, you will have a mass of 'raw' data and information. In general, analysis first requires that you familiarise yourself as much as possible with this information, 'immersing' yourself in the different interviewees' accounts. As part of this process you may find it useful to make summaries of each interview, noting major themes or consistent points of reference across the interviews conducted. It is the reporting and presentation of these summaries, often with quotations and extracts in support, that will comprise the final step of writing up. In the context of the research problem you commenced with, what have your interviewees told you about the topic under investigation?

 Activity 22.3

Choose one or more of the following research topics and practise your understanding of the stages involved in less formal interviews. Record any observations or notes.

a Conduct an informal interview with a colleague or friend on the subject of their life history and biography. Make careful notes or tape record their account. What have you learned about this person that you did not know before? Limit yourself to a 30 minute interview.

b Choose a particular commercial product sector – cars, beer, foods, cosmetics, coffees, etc. Carry out some exploratory interviews to assess attitudes and values associated with differing brands in that sector. Limit yourself to 30 minutes of interview time.

c Choose a particular event, preferably one which you did not attend. Build up a picture of the event – and different people's views of it – by means of less formal interviews. Try to complete at least three interviews.

d Give an account of two people's views on the state of the local and global environment using informal interview techniques.

Evaluate the outcome of your interviews.
- Did you succeed in gaining access to the information you wanted?
- How easy was it to synthesise and make sense of the information?
- Was this the best method to deal with the problem set?

23 Postscript

The following provides a summary of some of the key points raised in this part.

Recording interviews

There is considerable debate about the most effective ways of recording interviews. Researchers can use either one, or a combination of the following:

a prepared schedule completed by the interviewer;
b memory, with notes written up after the interview;
c notes written during the interview;
d tape recorder, from which transcripts may be made;
e video recorder, from which transcripts may be made.

All of these have their relative merits and drawbacks. Researchers opting for the formal survey approach (see Chapter 21), will tend to adopt the first of the above options. Those working with less formal techniques will favour the method which least intrudes into the interview by inhibiting the interviewee. Tape recording is the preferred method adopted here. Some attention should be given to the issue of recording the interviews well in advance of carrying them out.

Group interviews

We have been largely concerned with interview techniques in the context of single interviews with individual interviewees. It is important to note that researchers have also made use of interviews with groups of people. The benefits of this approach concern the potential for discussion to develop among the group and the value of this as a research source. Market researchers, for example, have employed 'focus groups' in their work. These are groups of consumers who are brought together by the interviewer to discuss and evaluate significant aspects of a given product range. In a similar fashion, other recent forms of social research have involved family groups, groups of school children or voters, for example.

There are some practical and organisational benefits as well; the group or sub-culture is often precisely what the researcher wants to investigate, and he or she may find it easier to gain access directly to the group – say at work or in a specific leisure location – than by contacting the individual members in turn.

Group interviews should therefore be considered, either as part of a survey or of a less formal type of interview project. One point to bear in mind if you decide to try group interviews concerns the particular dynamics of the group in question. Available research would suggest that group interviews may be less effective in allowing personal matters to emerge and that the interviewer will have to manage and be aware of the group dimensions in the conduct of the interview.

Summary and overview

Having read through the material and worked on the activities you should now be able to distinguish between different types of research interview practice. You should be able to evaluate the relative strengths and weaknesses of different styles of research interview and should have developed a sense of which types of interview are most appropriate for which types of research problem. In terms of your own projects, you should now be in a position to consider what interviews might offer you, and whether they are, as a result, worth employing and in what form.

Remember to bear in mind that the interview is a research technique, and that it will only generate information and data that is useful if you have used it appropriately, according to the specific aims and research objectives that you set yourself. You should be thinking about the types of data and information that your interviews will generate early in your project and how you will handle them as evidence for your conclusions as a whole. Two possibilities have been suggested:

a The first involves formal survey interviews and will be largely quantitative in scope and direction. Analysis of data will involve counting and identifying certain frequencies or patterns which emerge in your results. These patterns will be presented as the evidence for certain interpretations or conclusions. To support this, you would normally be expected to present your schedule of questions and a record of all the interviews carried out as part of your research report.

b The second involves a smaller number of less formal interviews, and aims at a more qualitative account of the topic or issue. In this case, the recorded material will not necessarily be reduced to statistical patterns. Instead, the accounts given by interviewees will be combed through for common themes or other points of significance. You may need to give more descriptive summaries of interviews and use quotations from them to support your analysis. In this way, interviewees are used as 'witnesses' in your presentation of the (or their) case. To support this, you should always be able to make full records of your interviews available. Remember, however, that you may wish to preserve the confidentiality of participants.

Now you should make a point of reviewing any notes that you may have made. If you are able to think about, organise and conduct better interviews, then this has been time and effort well spent. The acid test, however, lies ahead in the completion of your own projects.

24 Bibliography

Bell, J. (1987) *Doing your research project*, Milton Keynes, Open University Press.

Bilton, T. *et al* (eds) (1981) *Introductory sociology*, London, Macmillan.

Brennan, M. *et al* (eds) (1985) *The research interview: Uses and approaches*, London, Academic Press.

Cohen, L. and Mannion, L. (1989) *Research methods in education*, London, Routledge.

Hammersley, M. and Atkinson, P. (1983) *Ethnography: principles in practice*, London, Tavistock.

McCrossan, L. (1991) *A Handbook for interviewers* London, HMSO.

Moser, C. A. and Kalton, G. (1979) *Survey methods in social investigation*, London, Gower.

Oppenheim, A. N. (1992) *Questionnaire design, interviewing and attitude measurement*, Oxford, Blackwell.

Seidman, I. (1991) *Interviewing as qualitative research*, London, Teachers College Press.

Seldon, A. and Pappworth, J. (1983) *By word of mouth*, London, Methuen.

Walker, R. (ed.) (1985) *Applied qualitative research*, London, Gower.

In addition, you will find that most books on social research methods have sections on interviewing.

Lightning Source UK Ltd.
Milton Keynes UK
06 November 2009

145886UK00010B/1/P